Adam's Grief

To
Midway Community Covenant
Church

Cathy Sovold Johnson

Cathy Sovold Johnson

WESTBOW
PRESS®
A DIVISION OF THOMAS NELSON
& ZONDERVAN

On the cover: attributed to Carlo Magnone, Italian, 1623 - 1653
Adam Discovering the Body of Abel, date unknown / plausible date of c. 1644-1647
Oil on canvas
Minneapolis Institute of Art, The Putnam Dana McMillan Fund 72.84
Photo: Minneapolis Institute of Art

WestBow Press books may be ordered through booksellers or by contacting:

WestBow Press
A Division of Thomas Nelson & Zondervan
1663 Liberty Drive
Bloomington, IN 47403
www.westbowpress.com
1 (866) 928-1240

ISBN: 978-1-9736-1300-8 (sc)
ISBN: 978-1-9736-1301-5 (hc)
ISBN: 978-1-9736-1299-5 (e)

Library of Congress Control Number: 2017918683

Print information available on the last page.

WestBow Press rev. date: 01/09/2018

To Joel

Contents

Preface ix

Chapter 1 The Wake-Up Call 1
Chapter 2 They Got Our Attention: Now What? 13
Chapter 3 Some Background about Islam and
           Muslims 19
Chapter 4 How Are We to Respond to Islam? 27
Chapter 5 Early Muslim Expansion 35
Chapter 6 Islamic Extremism 43
Chapter 7 Religious Hatred and Violence 55
Chapter 8 Who Ya Gonna Hate? 63
Chapter 9 Allah 73
Chapter 10 Abraham 81
Chapter 11 Inclusion Versus Exclusion in the Bible
           and the Qur'an 89
Chapter 12 Immigrants and Refugees 99
Chapter 13 Love Is the Only Possible Answer 107
Chapter 14 What Can We Do? 117
Chapter 15 Receiving Muslim Hospitality 127
Chapter 16 The Tenacity of Hope 133

Endnotes 139
Bibliography 141

Preface

In a museum full of impressive art, hung high over a doorway, it would have been so easy to miss. Yet somehow it grabbed my attention, and continues to speak to me. It's a painting by an Italian painter named Carlo Magnone (1623–1653).

Although the painting is quite beautiful, it was not its beauty that grabbed my attention. Among all the paintings I walked past that day, this is the one I remember and continue to think about: *Adam Discovering the Body of Abel.*

The painting shows Adam, the bereaved, shocked, anguished father, bending over the dead body of his son Abel. In spite of having heard the story of Cain killing his brother, Abel, many times, I had never thought much about the pain suffered by Adam and Eve when one of their sons killed their other son.

The body of the slain Abel lies on the ground. The deed has been done. There is no hope of life. Murder cannot be undone. Abel is dead, and no amount of weeping, no amount of wishing, no amount even of praying can bring his body back to life.

And Cain. Cain has become a murderer. There is no way he can undo that which he has done. He cannot allow his anger to cool and change his plan to kill his brother. The action of murder leaves no opportunity for reconciliation between the brothers. Cain's brother is dead. Cain is left with only guilt and perhaps remorse.

Filled with grief, Adam drapes his body over the lifeless body of his son, Abel. Abel, in an act of worship, had just brought a lamb to sacrifice to God. Cain, also in an act of worship, had sacrificed some of the produce from his fields.

Cain's action against Abel was not only the first murder, but the first act of violence in the name of religion. The Genesis account of Cain and Abel leaves us with more questions than answers.

As I looked at that painting of the bereft Adam, mourning both the loss of his son Abel and the unthinkable action taken by his son Cain, I thought of how God must mourn over the violence of his children toward one another.

Although it's not clear in the passage exactly why God was displeased with Cain's sacrifice, God offered him another chance. After looking with favor on Abel's offering and withholding favor from Cain's offering, God said to Cain, "Why are you angry? Why is your face downcast? If you do what is right, will you not be accepted? But if you do not do what is right, sin is crouching at your door; it desires to have you, but you must master it" (Genesis 4:6–7).

In other words, God was offering Cain the opportunity to find redemption. Rather than choosing to accept God's offer, Cain slew his brother.

Hatred, murder, and war fill the pages of the history of humankind. Hatred, murder, and war continue to take top billing in the news today. And tragically, hatred, murder, and war are often entangled with religious differences.

Ever since the first murder when Cain killed Abel, apparently because he was jealous of his brother's sacrifice, religion has mingled with violence. The first murder was, as so many since then have been, a senseless murder. Adam, their father, embraces the lifeless body of his son, Abel. Adam grieves for the son whose life has been taken, and he grieves for the son who has become a murderer.

When God looks at his children today and sees hatred and wars, how God must grieve. When Jesus looked at the city of Jerusalem, he mourned over their hardness of heart, saying, "O Jerusalem, Jerusalem, you who kill the prophets and stone those sent to you, how often I have longed to gather your children together, as a hen gathers her chicks under her wings, but you were not willing" (Matthew 23:37 and Luke 13:34).

When our hearts are cold and hard toward our fellow humans, for whatever reason, God grieves. Since the beginning, humans have looked at one another and found differences that give us reason to hate. The Garden of Eden stories are so telling. Sin started with a piece of fruit. Really? Can that be possible? Yes, a piece of fruit! Then we have murder over a brother's jealousy concerning the sacrifice brought before God by his own brother! That's where it all started, and for time immemorial humans have looked at one another and decided it was their right to hate one another for every imaginable reason—from the color of their skin or shape of their eyes to the plot of ground they inhabit or their religious practices. And just as Adam grieved over his sons, God grieves when we choose to hate our sisters and brothers. For any reason.

Chapter 1

The Wake-Up Call

As part of one of my classes at Fuller Theological Seminary, I spent some time at the Seattle office of World Relief. A small group of us met with the director, Cal Uomoto. As he spoke with us, he opened my eyes to something in the Bible I had never seen. He led us on a journey through the Bible, pointing out what the scripture teaches about the stranger—the foreigner—the outsider.

He reminded us that God called Abraham to leave his country and his people and travel to a land God would show him. Abraham obeyed God, and he became a stranger in a foreign land. Later, Abraham's great-grandson, Joseph, was sold into slavery and taken to Egypt, where he was a stranger. After the death of Joseph, the Israelites were exiles, slaves in Egypt, a foreign land, for four hundred years.

Moses, who could have chosen to live a life of ease in Pharaoh's palace, led the Israelites out of Egypt and through the wilderness, where they wandered for forty years. When Moses was instructing the Israelites as to how they were to live in their new land, he reminded them that God "defends the cause of the fatherless and the widow, and loves the alien. ... And you are to love those who are aliens, for you yourselves were aliens in Egypt" (Deuteronomy 10:18–19).

There are more strangers on the list. Ruth, the young Moabite widow, left her homeland to go with Naomi to live in Bethlehem, where she was a foreigner. The result of the Babylonian captivity was that many, many Israelites were taken to live as captives in a foreign land. Among them was Daniel, a young man determined to honor God while living in exile in a pagan civilization. Another was Esther, a young woman growing up in a foreign land.

When Jesus was a young child, his parents fled with him to Egypt in order to protect him from the threats of Herod, a deranged despot. We love the story of Mary and Joseph finding a refuge in Bethlehem where Jesus could be born, but we often forget that they were soon forced to flee from their home, taking what must have been a difficult journey to Egypt, where they were foreigners— strangers in a foreign land.

This thread of strangers running through the Bible cannot be accidental. God loves the stranger. In fact, Jesus says that the way we treat the stranger is the way God will judge us: "For I was hungry and you gave me nothing to eat, I was thirsty and you gave me nothing to drink, I was a stranger and you did not invite me in" (Matthew 25:42–43). In essence, the way we treat the stranger is the way we treat Jesus. Jesus warns, "I tell you the truth, whatever you did not do for one of the least of these, you did not do for me" (Matthew 25:45). In Hebrews 13:2, we are reminded, "Do not forget to entertain strangers, for by so doing some people have entertained angels without knowing it."

God's love for all peoples is clear in the message of salvation through Jesus Christ offered to all people: "For God so loved the world that he gave his one and only Son, that whoever believes in him shall not perish but have eternal life" (John 3:16). This vision is realized in the words of Revelation: "After this I looked and there before me was a great multitude that no one could count, from every nation, tribe, people and language, standing before the throne and in front of the Lamb" (Revelation 7:9). What a beautiful, glorious hope!

Listening to these examples of biblical teaching on the foreigner, the alien, and the stranger, woven throughout scripture was, for me, an eye-opener. I knew all of these scriptures, but I had never seen it as a theme. Strangers, immigrants, refugees, aliens—whether undocumented or not—are people who are loved by God.

In the book of Deuteronomy, the Israelites are reminded that they are called to be different because of who their God is. One of those differences is in how they treat the people they think of as outsiders. The Israelites knew themselves as God's chosen people. So naturally, they assumed God loved them best. We Christians have inherited that from them, haven't we? Now, we assume that God loves us best!

The Israelites wanted to be their own nation and have their own land. Even so, they kept running into all these foreigners. Foreigners surrounded them and even lived among them.

Living in a time of tribes and small nations, the default way of behaving toward other tribes and nations was sometimes to tolerate one another and more often to wage war against one another. So, what we read in Deuteronomy is startling.

This small, struggling nomadic nation was called to something that can only be seen as shocking. Here's what God told his people:

> For the Lord your God is God of gods and Lord of lords, the great God, mighty and awesome, who shows no partiality and accepts no bribes. He defends the cause of the fatherless and the widow, and loves [not tolerates; loves!] the foreigner residing among you, giving them food and clothing. And you are to love those who are foreigners, for you yourselves were foreigners in Egypt.
> (Deuteronomy 10:17–19)

If we actually believe the Bible, this tells us that God loves not only us but those we might think of as our enemies—or at least not our friends. People who are certainly not one of us.

As followers of Jesus, it matters greatly to us what Jesus said. Jesus actually takes the commandments in the Old Testament one step further and claims that the way we treat strangers is the way we treat him. Jesus so closely identifies with the stranger and the person in need that when we mistreat them, he tells us we are mistreating him. Jesus said, "For I was hungry and you gave me something to eat, I was thirsty and you gave me something to drink, I was a stranger and you invited me in, I needed clothes and you clothed me, I was sick and you looked after me, I was in prison and you came to visit me" (Matthew 25:35–36).

Paul echoes this thought in Romans:

> Bless those who persecute you; bless and do not curse. Rejoice with those who rejoice; mourn with those who mourn. Live in harmony with one another. Do not be proud, but be willing to associate with people of low position. Do not be conceited. Do not repay anyone evil for evil. Be careful to do what is right in the eyes of everyone. If it is possible, as far as it depends on you, live at peace with everyone. Do not take revenge, my dear friends, but leave room for God's wrath, for it is written: "It is mine to avenge; I will repay," says the Lord. On the contrary: "If your enemy is hungry, feed him; if he is thirsty, give him something to drink. In doing this, you will heap burning coals on his head." Do not be overcome by evil, but overcome evil with good. (Romans 12:14–21)

As I listened to these and other scriptures, I was surprised. I had heard them all before, but I had never heard them together. I had never thought about this as an important theme of caring for the stranger running through the Bible. Clearly, that day God was opening my eyes to something new in scripture.

Mr. Uomoto also explained the difference between refugees and immigrants. Immigrants make a decision, for any number of reasons, to migrate to a new place. My Norwegian forbears were immigrants. Times were tough in their homeland, and they decided to take a chance on America. Refugees, on the other hand, are people who have been forced to leave their homelands either by extreme living conditions or by political persecution. In order to be called a refugee, a person's status must be determined by the United Nations High Commission for Refugees (UNHCR). Established in 1951, the Refugee Convention defines a refugee as a person who is outside his or her country of nationality or habitual residence; has a well-founded fear of being persecuted because of his or her race, religion, nationality, membership of a particular social group or political opinion; and is unable or unwilling to avail him- or herself of the protection of that country, or to return there, for fear of persecution (see Article 1A(2)).[1]

Refugees, in other words, are forced to move in order to save their lives or preserve their freedom. Refugees are screened and selected by the UNHCR and placed in countries that are willing to receive them.

Agencies like World Relief receive the refugees, who usually arrive in the United States with not much more than the clothes on their backs and maybe a small suitcase. World Relief works primarily with individuals and churches who agree to sponsor refugees. With a representative from World Relief, the sponsor meets the refugees at the airport and then hosts them in their home, usually for about three weeks, until they can be situated in their own apartment. Currently in the Seattle area, refugees usually go directly to their own housing since there are insufficient homes available to host them.

The next time I went to World Relief, I was sitting with Kelly, a World Relief staff member. She showed me the paperwork for a young couple who would be arriving in Seattle in a couple of days. They were already on their way, and World Relief would meet them at the airport, but Kelly had not yet found a home in which to place them. They were a husband and wife, in their midtwenties, from Somalia. They had fled from Somalia to Pakistan, where they had been living for several years in a refugee camp. They were Muslims.

As I looked at their papers, I was immediately certain that God was calling me to welcome these strangers into my home. With only the youngest of our three children still living at home, we had the space. I made a phone call, and my husband quickly agreed this was something we should do. The plan was that they would stay with us for three weeks, and then World Relief workers would help them move into an apartment.

Hearing that they were Muslims did not concern me. The year was 2001, and as far as I knew, I had never met a Muslim, nor did I know much about what Muslims believed. Even as I looked forward to meeting them and learning about them, I thought perhaps through our welcoming them and telling them about the gospel, they might even want to become Christians.

A few days later, along with Kelly from World Relief, we met them at the Seattle-Tacoma Airport. They were attractive and polite, and having traveled so far, very tired. I was relieved to hear them speak to us in English. Each of them came with a suitcase filled with all of their belongings. Kelly came with them to our home to help ease the settling-in process. I was grateful for her presence. She had explained to me that they would not be familiar with our Western bathrooms, and when using the toilet, they would want to clean themselves, not with toilet paper, but using a pitcher of water. This was pretty strange to me. Kelly led them into our bathroom and gave them instructions as to how to use all of the fixtures. I was glad when she handed them a towel and said, "Americans like to keep their floors dry."

That's for sure, I thought, wondering what other surprises there might be in the coming weeks.

Their names were Ali and Ubah, and we got along fine. Ali was energetic and social. Ubah wore lovely scarves and spoke with a soft, musical voice. They kept the bathroom floor dry. The first Sunday, we invited them to go to church with us. Ubah declined, but Ali went and seemed to enjoy himself. I asked Ali about their religion, Islam. He explained to me that he really didn't know much of anything about Islam, because the Qur'an is written in Arabic, and he doesn't speak Arabic, so he has never read it. Nevertheless, he considered himself to be a Muslim.

At first, this shocked me. But as I pondered it, I realized that most likely there are, and have been over the centuries, many Christians who really know little or nothing of what's in the Bible. Having grown up in evangelical churches, where so much emphasis is placed on biblical teaching, this was an interesting thing for me to think about. Do you need to know the Bible in order to be a Christian?

Ali had a little book with many phone numbers, and he spent quite a bit of time making contact with friends. One day, a Somali couple came to our home to visit them. All of their conversation was in Somali. I sensed that the Somali visitors were not very warm toward us, and perhaps they were even warning Ali and Ubah not to be overly friendly with us. After that visit, it seemed to me Ali and Ubah were just a little more guarded. The following Sunday, they were no longer willing to go to church with us. Even though they continued to be polite, it seemed as if they were just a bit more distant with us.

When the time came to move them into their apartment, it was somewhat of a relief. It was not that we didn't like them or didn't want to see them again, but the time was right. We knew how eager they were to have their own place. World Relief had found them an apartment close to the Seattle-Tacoma Airport because Ali said his friends had told him he could easily find a job working in security at the airport.

One week after we moved them into their apartment, I woke up to the news on the radio that a hijacked airplane had crashed into the Twin Towers of the World Trade Center in New York City. I ran and turned on the television, and I watched with shock as a second plane hit the second tower, a third plane hit the Pentagon, and a fourth plane crashed to the ground in Pennsylvania. If you're old enough to remember September 11, 2001, you most likely remember exactly how you learned about that terrifying moment in our history.

No experience in my lifetime had been anything like it. Like every other American, I watched these events unfold on the screen in total disbelief and horror. The tragedy was monumental. In the days and weeks that followed, like every other American, I asked "Why? Who are these people who committed these heinous acts? Why would anyone want to do such a thing?" And over and over, I asked, "Why do they hate us so much? Why, in fact, would they hate us enough to give their lives?"

In the days following the attacks, we learned that the perpetrators were Muslims. I realized that the sum of my knowledge about Muslims would easily fit on an index card. In my mind, Muslims and Arabs and Middle Easterners were synonymous. I had long ago given up trying to understand Arab political issues. I remember seeing Arabs on newscasts with what looked to me like dishtowels on their heads. How could they possibly expect to be taken seriously dressing that way? Don't they realize people don't dress that way anymore? And, I am not proud to say, I pretty much concluded that if "those people" in the Middle East wanted to continually blow one another up, that was their problem and not mine.

But now, things had changed. To begin with, I was party to bringing a Muslim couple into our country, and I really knew very little about them. It was important for me to know who Muslims really were, what they believed, and why they had launched such a horrific attack on the United

States. Our nation had been blindsided by an attack—not on a battlefield but an attack against innocent civilians. Children, firefighters, office workers, and travelers had been killed by a terrorist attack. This time, the "why" questions refused to leave me alone.

Chapter 2

They Got Our Attention: Now What?

Tragedy shatters our peaceful innocence, leaving us feeling vulnerable and unsafe. It rarely seems to make sense. In the years since 9/11, we have become accustomed to being searched, questioned, and even patted down in order to board an airplane. We have gotten used to news reports of Islamic terrorist acts in places where we used to feel completely safe. Terrorism has robbed us of our sense that the world is, for the most part, a decent, kind, safe, and orderly place. Today, terrorism, both here in the United States and around the world, seems to be a never-ending reality.

One of the puzzling aspects of terrorism is that it seems to lack all reason. The victims are no better or worse than any of the rest of us—they simply happen to be in the wrong place at the wrong time. The result is a level of dis-ease we feel, knowing that, while most of us will never be the victims of Islamic terrorists, we can't know for sure. We can't know where or when the next act of terrorism will take place or who the victims will be. The randomness of terrorism succeeds in instilling fear where we never felt fear before. Something could happen at any time or any place to anyone. And it might be me.

In the days and weeks following 9/11, I kept asking myself questions: Why do they hate us? Why, in fact, do they hate us so very much that they would sacrifice their own lives in order to wreak havoc and destruction, murdering innocents? What do we even have to do with this?

The more I thought about it, the more I realized just how completely ignorant I was concerning issues in the Middle East and the religion of Islam. Since I was, at the time, working on a master of divinity degree in theology, I was particularly interested in the religious aspect of the issue.

I noticed some Christians were beginning to make attempts to engage in interfaith dialogue between Christians and Muslims. I also noticed that, as far as I could see, Evangelicals—the part of the Christian Church I identify with—were, for the most part, missing from that table of dialogue. Also, though most people were simply silent on the issue, Evangelical Christians seemed more likely to be speaking hatefully toward Muslims rather than wanting to engage them in dialogue.

My own first reaction was to remain silent, hoping to puzzle myself through this very tragic and terrible event of world history. I simply did not have the background to know how to even grapple with it. The unthinkable had happened, and my mind could not quite process this unfathomable event. My limited, Western-biased understanding of world history was not sufficient to help me really understand the meaning of this event. Things I assumed to be true were no longer necessarily true. In short, my worldview had been sideswiped—knocked off its axis—and I could not figure out what to think.

I think many Americans were, and still are, like me. We want to understand, but this is beyond us. It is as if there is a huge gap in our understanding of the world. We thought we understood the world, but we suddenly realize that our understanding is woefully inadequate. Either the world changed while we were not paying attention, our understanding of the world was far more limited than we realized, or—most likely—both.

As a result, I began to look for ways of educating myself on the religion of Islam and the countries in the Middle East. I was hoping to be able to understand the mind-set of terrorists. I know a lot more now than I did then, but I also realize that the problems are complex, and as A. A. Milne's character Winnie-the-Pooh so wisely put it, "I am a Bear of Very Little Brain, and long words bother me."[2] The answers are not simple.

I want to be clear that even though I subsequently engaged in a weeklong Christian-Muslim intensive seminar at Georgetown University, I have visited several mosques, I have written a dissertation on the subject of Christian-Muslim dialogue for which I earned a doctor of ministry degree from San Francisco Theological Seminary, I continue to make attempts to engage in dialogue with my neighbors who are Muslims, and I continue to read on the subject, I confess I still have much to learn. I know a lot more than I did. Still, I write, not as an expert, but as a learner who wants to encourage others to think along with me and grapple with how to respond to the world we live in as Christians seeking to live according to biblical teachings.

I write also as a Christian who is convinced that the Bible is relevant to today's issues. Of course, the Bible is a big book, written long ago. In order to understand scripture, we need to read it with some understanding of the context in which it was written, carefully and prayerfully interpreting it as it applies to us today. For example, while the truth of the Golden Rule—"Do unto others as you would have them do unto you"—transcends all times and cultures, the dietary rules given to the Israelites when they were wandering in the wilderness probably are not applicable to most Christians today. This understanding of the diversity of material in the Bible in no way demeans the concept of truth in scripture. Rather, it is a reminder that we need to read with discernment.

I call myself an Evangelical Christian, but I sometimes bristle at the media's use of the term *Evangelical*, which lumps all Evangelical Christians into a particular mindset and even a voting bloc. This is an oversimplification. An Evangelical Christian is one who believes that Jesus, as presented in the Bible, is good news for the world. *Evangelical* comes from the Greek word *euangelion*, which means "good news," and is often translated in the Bible as *gospel*. Christians believe the good news is that Jesus came into the world in order to bring the *euangelion* that God loves the people of this world. All of them.

If ever this world needed good news, it is now. Sadly, Evangelicals have managed to get a reputation today of being rigid, judgmental, and downright hateful toward all sorts of people, including Muslims. While some Evangelicals may deserve this reputation, certainly most do not. Rather than understanding *Evangelical* as good news, many people today hear the word and think it means "Bad news, sinner! You're going to hell!" Religion today is often seen as divisive and hateful rather than inclusive and loving. Why is this? How did this happen? Or has it always been this way?

When I was a child, growing up immersed in an Evangelical church, I learned to sing, "Jesus loves the little children, all the children of the world ..." I assumed that "all" meant "all." I assumed that Jesus loved all of the children, and by extension, their fathers and mothers as well, regardless of skin color, nationality, or even religion. I thought it meant that God was the God of the entire world.

There was, however, a caveat to this universal love of God. Evangelicalism brought with it a parallel message of condemnation toward all who reject the message of salvation through Jesus Christ. I believe it is time for us to take a closer look at the message of condemnation. We Christians should never be afraid to ask questions or reexamine our beliefs. We have an amazing God who is not threatened by our deepest questions. We should never be afraid to search the scriptures to make sure that what we believe is actually the message found in the Bible.

Does the Bible really teach that my neighbors who are Muslims are beyond the circle of God's love? We can ask this question, of course, about Jews, Buddhists, atheists, and many others who are not Christian, but for the purpose of this book, we will be talking about Muslims in particular. I will say more about this in chapter 7, but before we go further with this question, maybe we should get to know our Muslim neighbors a little better.

Chapter 3

Some Background about Islam and Muslims

Islam is the religion begun by the prophet Muhammad. People who follow the religion of Islam are known as Muslims. Compared to other major world religions, Islam is rather young. Judaism dates back to Abraham, who lived sometime around 2100–1900 BC. Hinduism began around 1500 BC, and Buddhism began around 560 BC. Christianity is easier to date because our Western calendar is based on the birth of Christ. Christianity is said to begin around AD 30, when Jesus began his ministry. Islam was instituted by Muhammad, who lived from AD 570–632 in what today is Saudi Arabia. By the time of Muhammad, both Christians and Jews had been dispersed throughout the Mediterranean world. Relative to each other, Judaism is the oldest religion, Christianity is next, and Islam began about six hundred years after the birth of Christianity.

When he was forty years old, Muhammad received his first revelation in a cave near Mecca, in present-day Saudi Arabia. At that time, although there were some Jews and

Christians in Arabia, the vast majority of the population were polytheists—idol worshippers. Muhammad began teaching the people that they must stop worshipping idols and only worship the one true God, Allah. It's important to note that Muhammad did not invent the word *Allah*. Rather, Allah is the word for *God* in Arabic, so Jews and Christians who speak Arabic also use the word *Allah* to mean God.

Muhammad was in the habit of going to a cave to meditate, and it was while he was in the cave that he received what he claimed were prophecies from Allah (God), brought to him by the archangel, Gabriel. Muhammad was a merchant. It is generally believed that Muhammad was illiterate or at least partially illiterate. As a merchant, he probably was able to write numbers and a few words, but he may not have been able to write his thoughts. So, when he received the prophecies, he recited them, and others recorded them. Eventually, after his death, his recitations were formulated into the Qur'an. Muhammad's central message was that the people should reject all of their gods and worship Allah alone. Just as the Bible is the holy book of Christians, the Qur'an is the holy book for all Muslims.

Like Jews and Christians, Muslims trace their roots back to Abraham. This is why Judaism, Christianity, and Islam are sometimes called the Abrahamic faiths. While Jews and Christians trace their lineage back to Abraham through his son, Isaac, Muslims trace their roots back to Abraham through his son, Ishmael, who was born to the slave woman, Hagar. Perhaps you remember the story in the Bible about Hagar.

In Genesis 12:1–2, and again in Genesis 15, God promised Abraham that he would make of him a great nation. However, as the years went by, Abraham's wife, Sarah, failed to conceive and have a child. So, although God had promised Abraham that he would be the father of a great nation, there was no heir. In light of their age and the fact that there was still no heir, Sarah offered her Egyptian maidservant, Hagar, to Abraham. Not surprising, Sarah became resentful toward Hagar and abused her, so that she ran away. But an angel of the Lord came to Hagar and told her to go back to Sarah and submit to her. The angel told Hagar she would have a son who she would name Ishmael. The angel went on to say, "He will be a wild donkey of a man; his hand will be against everyone and everyone's hand against him, and he will live in hostility toward all his brothers" (Genesis 16:12). So, when Abraham (still known at this time as Abram) was eighty-six years old, Hagar bore him a son, Ishmael.

Some thirteen years later, God again appeared to Abraham, making a covenant with him and telling him he would be the father of many nations. He also told Abraham, who was now ninety-nine years old, that he would bear a son by his wife, Sarah, who was now ninety years old. This was when Sarah made God angry by laughing. It's interesting to note that Abraham also laughed (Genesis 17:17), but it was Sarah's laughter that angered God (Genesis 18:10–15). Sarah then gave birth to a son, named Isaac, and Isaac became the legal heir. This, of course, caused more strife between the two women: Sarah, Abraham's wife and the mother of Isaac, and Hagar, the slave who was mother of Ishmael.

On the day Sarah's son, Isaac, was weaned, Abraham gave a great feast. But Sarah was not happy because of the presence of Hagar's son, Ishmael. She told Abraham to get rid of Hagar and Ishmael. God told the distressed Abraham that he should allow Sarah to send Hagar away, but that Ishmael would also father a nation. Abraham gave Hagar some provisions and sent her and the boy away into the desert.

When the provisions ran out, Hagar and her son, Ishmael, sat down in the desert and waited to die. Then God heard the boy crying and spoke to Hagar, promising that God would make the boy into a great nation, and provided them with a well of water. "God was with the boy as he grew up. He lived in the desert and became an archer. While he was living in the Desert of Paran, his mother got a wife for him from Egypt" (Genesis 21:20–21).

The Bible does not tell any more about Ishmael's life until we are told that Abraham died at the age of 175 and was buried by his sons Isaac and Ishmael (Genesis 25:7–10). Following this statement, there is a paragraph naming Ishmael's twelve sons and concluding, "And they lived in hostility toward all their brothers" (Genesis 25:13–18).

According to Muslim tradition, at some time after Hagar had fled into the wilderness with her son, Ishmael, Abraham learned that Hagar and Ishmael were alive, and he went to find them. He found them in what is today the city of Mecca. Together, Abraham and Ishmael rebuilt the Kaaba, a temple to the one true God. Muslims believe that the Kaaba, a large black cube that contains the sacred Black Stone, had originally been built by Adam. The Kaaba is the center of worship for Muslims around the world today, the place in Mecca where every Muslim wants to go at least once in his or her lifetime.

By the time of Muhammad, in the late sixth and early seventh century AD, the Kaaba was being used as a shrine for the tribal idols and gods of Arabia. Muhammad entered Mecca, cleansed the Kaaba of its 360 idols, and restored the "religion of Abraham," the worship of the one true God.

Muslims observe the five pillars of Islam. The first pillar is that all Muslims testify to the Declaration of Faith, which says, "There is no god but God (Allah), and Muhammad is the messenger of God."

The second pillar is prayer. Muslims pray five times each day: at daybreak, noon, midafternoon, sunset, and evening. Muslims always face Mecca when they pray, and they always begin with the "Allahu Akbar," which means "God is most great." The prayers are a very important part of Muslim life, and in many parts of the world, you will hear the prayers recited over loudspeakers coming from the towers of the mosques.

The third pillar is "Zakat," which means purification. Zakat is an expression of a Muslim's worship and thanksgiving to God by supporting the poor. It requires an annual contribution of 2.5 percent of a person's wealth and assets, not merely a percentage of annual income.

The fourth pillar is Ramadan. Once a year, during the month of Ramadan, Muslims abstain from dawn to sunset from food, drink, and sexual activity, health permitting. Each night during Ramadan, Muslims break their fast with the call to prayer, followed by a meal called Iftar.

The fifth pillar is the Hajj, the pilgrimage to Mecca. Mecca, a city in Saudi Arabia, is the place where the religion of Islam began, and it is the place Muslims around the world face each day when they recite their prayers. It is also the place every Muslim aspires to visit at least once in his or her lifetime. Every year following Ramadan, somewhere between 1.5 and 3 million Muslims from all over the world travel to Mecca for the Hajj, where they walk around the Kaaba.

The mosque is the Muslim place of worship, the equivalent of the Christian church or the Jewish synagogue. Like churches, mosques range from those that are huge and opulently decorated to those that are small and very simple. If you haven't seen many mosques, I encourage you to look online at pictures of mosques. You might notice that mosques do not have pictures of people or animals because of Muslims' belief that they are expressions that lead to idolatry, but instead often have intricate patterns and ornate calligraphy. It is extremely important in Islam to avoid anything whatsoever that would be seen as a form of idolatry.

The mosque is the place where Muslims gather to worship and pray. Muslims pray five times a day, every day, and whenever possible, they gather in their mosques for their prayers. If you have the opportunity to visit a mosque, you should know that upon entering, you will be expected to remove your shoes, and women will be expected to cover their heads. I have visited the Blue Mosque in Istanbul. It is amazingly beautiful and huge and has ornate tilework. The most memorable thing about that mosque, for me, is the carpet, which seems to stretch forever. The oriental-style carpet's woven pattern is designed in rows that designate spots for each person who has come to pray. I have also visited the Islamic center in my neighborhood, which is rather small. From the outside, it looks like a simple, modern office building, but it functions like a mosque as a place for Muslims to gather and to pray.

As Muslims gather in the mosque, the men arrange themselves in rows, shoulder to shoulder. They generally begin by sitting on the floor and listening to a reading from the Qur'an in Arabic, which is sometimes a recording, and a teaching given by the Imam or another leader. They stand in unison and kneel in unison, and at certain times in their prayers, they bow with their foreheads to the ground. The women gather behind the men, sometimes lining up in a similar manner to the men and sometimes seated in chairs at the back. It has been explained to me that the reason the women stay behind the men is for the purpose of the modesty of the women.

The towers or spires on mosques are called minarets. Originally, these minarets were used to cool the building, drawing the hot air out through the minaret. Today, minarets are used as a tower from which the community hears the call to prayer, called the Adhan. The call to prayer is sung in Arabic, projected either by a singer who has the ability to sing loudly or by using a loudspeaker. Today, the call to prayer is often a recording.

Some people, particularly non-Muslims, find these five-times-daily calls to prayer to be loud, offensive, and annoying. I admit I have never lived next to one for an extended time, but I love to hear the call to prayer, the

Adhan, because being called to stop and pray is a beautiful invitation, even though I do not understand the Arabic words. It's a reminder to me as a Christian that there are things we can learn from people of different faiths. The discipline of pausing five times a day, every day, to pray impresses and challenges me. I have also heard people complain that church bells are loud, offensive, and annoying, and I have a hard time understanding that as well.

There are two major divisions in Islam: Sunni and Shii. This division dates back to the death of Muhammad in AD 632. When Muhammad died, he had not chosen a successor, which led to a disagreement as to who would succeed him as the leader of this new religion. Because Muhammad did not have a son, the question as to who should succeed him was divisive. Some believed the successor should be the person who was best qualified to lead, while others believed the succession should be determined by heredity. Those who favored heredity chose Ali, who was the husband of Muhammad's daughter, Fatima. Ali's followers became the part of Islam called Shii, also known as Shiites, while those who favored choosing the successor by his qualifications became the Sunnis. Shiites and Sunnis are still the two major divisions in Islam. Today, 85 percent of Muslims are Sunni, and 15 percent are Shii. There is also a mystical approach to Islam called Sufism. Sufis emphasize "the 'interior' path, seeking the purity and simplicity of the time of Muhammad, as the route to the direct and personal experience of God."[3]

Chapter 4

How Are We to Respond to Islam?

In my lifetime, Muslims have gone from being people of a religion that most Christians in America know little or nothing about to being in the news almost every day. In recent years, many Muslims have migrated to the United States. In many parts of our country, it's no longer unusual to see a woman wearing a hijab, the headscarf that many Muslim women wear for modesty. The same is true in much of Europe.

This change has been quite rapid. I still remember, just a few years ago, an occasion when I was shopping in a large department store in a mall in the Seattle area. When I brought my purchase to the cash register, the clerk was a young woman wearing a hijab that covered all of her hair. Even though this was after I had hosted Muslims in my own home and had begun studying about Muslims, it was still startling. It quite simply challenged my own stereotype of what a sales clerk was "supposed" to look like. It reminded me that the world was changing, and it forced me to think more about my own prejudices.

Today, of the 6.8 million people in the world, somewhere between 1.9 and 2.1 billion are Christian, and 1.6 billion are Muslim. Some put it at 33 percent Christian and from 21 to 23 percent Muslim, with the Christian population in decline and the Muslim population growing.[4]

The terrorist attack of 9/11 got the attention of Americans. That day, we as a nation lost our innocent naïveté. No longer could we hear about conflicts in the Middle East and yawn and go back to our secure lives, safe in the assumption that none of this mattered to us. Our world had been rocked, and we now knew that something was very wrong. I wanted to understand who the perpetrators were and why they were so angry. As I tried to understand, I became overwhelmed by the complexity of Middle Eastern history and current political issues. If issues of Middle Eastern history were taught when I was in school, I must have slept through it (entirely possible!).

There is a humorous map that shows the United States from the viewpoint of a New Yorker, in which New York City occupies most of the space, and the rest of the country is sort of squeezed around the edges. I confess that the worldview I grew up with would look somewhat like that. The United States would, of course, be in the center, with Canada and Mexico above and below, but very small. The eastern edge of the map would consist of Europe and the biblical Israel fairly prominent. There would be some smaller representations of Russia, China, and Japan, the mission fields of Africa and South America, the North Pole with Santa Claus, and the South Pole with a few penguins. And the Middle East? Pretty much missing. Just a giant desert wasteland beyond the edge of Israel.

Both my perception of the world and the reality of the world have changed in the past fifteen years. The Middle East refuses to be ignored. The religion of Islam refuses be ignored. Muslim people can no longer be ignored. They are on our streets and sitting beside our children in school. They are migrating in droves from the Middle East and Africa, and we have witnessed horrific pictures of Muslim refugees drowning in the Mediterranean Sea. The beautiful Mediterranean's blue waters have become a hideous grave where men, women, and children have lost their lives trying desperately to escape chaos and destruction that is almost beyond our comprehension. Whole cities in the Middle East have been virtually destroyed. Europe vacillates between welcoming the refugees and wanting to send them back—and so does the United States. It seems as if every day, somewhere in the United States or Europe, there is news of an Islamic terrorist attack. Senseless murders shatter our peaceful existence and leave us on edge.

Can you blame us for being angry? We know the world has always known wars and rumors of wars, but this is crazy! This is just plain wrong! It feels as if some cruel and unpredictable evil is lurking about, infiltrating our communities, and threatening to attack us at any moment. It's as if an insidious, fatal disease has infiltrated our world—and we have no idea where it will strike next.

We realize, with a certain amount of despair, that we don't know how to fix this problem. Our national and international leaders point fingers at one another and promise solutions, but it seems like no one knows what to do. The result is a general dis-ease, a feeling that all is not well in our land. Many Americans are feeling a confusing mixture of fear and anger. There is lots of blame going around. Maybe a bit of confused guilt. Things are just not right, so we look around for someone—anyone—to blame.

And look. There they are, walking down the main streets of Anytown, USA, wearing headscarves and acting as if this is their home! It's really not surprising that many Americans harbor ill will toward Muslim immigrants and refugees. Politicians bicker publicly as to whether we should be welcoming Muslims into our country or vetting newcomers more carefully or sending them back where they came from, as if that were even possible.

What should be the Christian response? Does the biblical mandate to love our neighbor mean we should open our arms to Muslims? Or does the danger of Islamic terrorism change things to the extent that these people do not deserve our love? Is it okay for a Christian to hate certain people?

The Bible tells us to love our enemies. But what about war? Doesn't the reality of war allow us to hate our enemies? And if not, how then is a soldier capable of killing the enemy, thereby protecting his or her country?

The pacifist would argue that war is never justifiable, so killing even the enemy is not an option. The majority of Christians, however, believe that war for the purpose of protecting one's country is justifiable. While there is a broad spectrum of thinking as to how and when our nation ought to be engaged in wars, most people agree that the use of military strength for the purpose of protecting our nation against aggression by another nation is sometimes necessary.

What does the Bible have to say about war? In some ways, a lot, and in other ways, not much. There are lots and lots of battles in the Bible. In the Old Testament accounts, it seems that God is always on the side of the Israelites. God leads them into battle, and God cheers for them in battle and brings them victories. These battles are not only for their protection. The Israelites, with God's encouragement, invade other nations who happen to be living in the part of the world that God has told them is to be their home—their promised land.

Christians reading the Old Testament today have different ways of understanding this account of a God who seems to favor war. Some would argue that at that time in history, the only way for the Israelites to live at peace was to wipe out their godless, idolatrous enemies. They would say God had given them the promised land, and it was their right to rid the land of all who lived there. Others would argue that it is still the right of the Jews, the descendants of Abraham and Sarah (but not the descendants of Abraham and Hagar) to defend their land. Other Christians would question this, wondering whether or not God actually sanctioned all of the bloodshed, both in biblical times and today.

Historically, the Bible has been used to argue both in support of war and against war. It is not my intent in this book to argue for or against Christian pacifism. I know and respect people on both sides of this issue. Further, the complexity of each situation may lead to different positions. My purpose here is to contribute to the discussion of how we as Christians are going to respond to Muslims in our midst and to the changes in our world politically, with respect to Islam. As an ordinary, not-very-political citizen, my concern is primarily how I relate to my Muslim neighbors. However, as a citizen of the United States, I also need to think carefully about how my country relates to Muslims, both here in America and in the theater of world politics.

There's a wonderful song that begins, "Let there be peace on earth, and let it begin with me." Each of us begins with our own actions in our own community, but we also are voters in a democracy, so we need to think not only locally, but also nationally and globally. It would be so much easier to hide our heads in the sand and pretend this issue doesn't matter, but peace on earth begins with each one of us.

Still, peace is not so easy. In the larger context of our world, the issues concerning conflict between nations and peoples have become much more complex. Today, scenes of war on the other side of the globe are on our televisions in our homes. We may say that peace begins at home, with the neighbor who lives next to us, and that is true. But like it or not, we are citizens not only of our communities and our nations but of the world. Most of us don't think of ourselves as influential in world politics. However, in recent years, the world has shown up on our doorsteps, often in the form of immigrants and refugees in our communities. The political upheaval around the world has an impact on us whether we realize it or not. Even if you don't happen to have refugees in your neighborhood, you have the responsibility as a citizen and a voter to think carefully about how you will respond to this changing world.

One way to begin is by learning more about the issues and the people. Another way is by thinking carefully about your own religious beliefs and how they should be interpreted in your own life, in your church, in your community, and in your nation. In the next two chapters, we will look at early Muslim expansion and Muslim extremism in order to better understand the underlying issues facing us today.

Chapter 5

Early Muslim Expansion

I grew up thinking that history was a boring subject full of wars that I thought had nothing to do with me. It seemed to be a matter of facts and dates and names of dead people and wars that I never understood and cared about even less. Even now, I confess that I find writing a chapter concerning history daunting. However, I have learned that history, especially when it does not require me to face exams filled with what I considered meaningless names and dates, is actually very interesting. And it does matter. It matters a great deal.

History has shaped much of what I believe about myself, about government, and about God. It is true that I am a Christian because I choose to be a Christian, but my decision has also been highly influenced by the time and place and circumstance of my birth. My decision to be a Christian was partially made possible by historical events that happened centuries before I was born. I may think I made this decision on my own, but the truth is that many events of history outside of myself made my decision possible.

History is much more than a set of irrefutable facts and dates. Historical accounts and interpretations vary widely, depending on who is telling the story. Think, for example, of your own family history. If something touchy or controversial happened in your family, different family members might tell the story differently. And those outside of your family might have an even different way of telling the story. When you think about history as a story of the past told from a certain viewpoint, it becomes much more interesting. When you read history, you need to consider who is telling the story and why they have chosen to tell it in the way they are presenting it. That is how it is with the history of Muslim expansion. The same can be said concerning Christian expansion, of course, but that's another story.

The first time I began to think about Muslim expansion was when I looked at the maps in the textbook that was used for my Early Church History seminary class, which was, of course, about the history of Christian expansion. The first chapter of Christian expansion, of course, is in the Bible, where we read the accounts in Acts about the beginnings of the church, and we read the letters written by Paul, which give us glimpses into his missionary journeys. My church history textbook explained that, during the first century, Christianity spread "by the countless and nameless Christians who for different reasons—persecution, business, or missionary calling—traveled from place to place taking the news of the Gospel with them."[5]

In the first century, the Roman Empire stretched from what today is England, south to northern Africa, to the Near East, including what is modern-day Turkey. To put it simply, the Roman Empire included all of the land surrounding the Mediterranean Sea.

During the first centuries of Christian history, Christians were a persecuted people in the Roman Empire. However, in AD 306, Constantine became the emperor. Under Constantine, Christians went from being persecuted to being favored by the Roman Empire. In AD 313, Constantine issued the Edict of Milan, which meant that it was no longer a crime to practice Christianity. Constantine was baptized on his deathbed in AD 337. In AD 380, the Edict of Thessalonica declared Christianity to be the state religion of the Roman Empire. This means that in a period of only about two generations, Christians in the Roman Empire went from being persecuted for their faith to being part of the dominant culture. Christianity was now the official religion of the Roman Empire.

If you picture the map of the Roman Empire, all of that territory stretching from what is today England to Egypt was Christian. It is a little difficult for our modern minds to understand what it means for the state to declare to its subjects what their religion shall now be. We can't help but wonder what the average citizen thought or believed. Okay, folks, we know that your grandparents watched while the emperor threw the Christians to the lions, but now, we're not only going to be kind to Christians, but you are all now officially Christians. The emperor has declared it, and it is so. You are now subjects of the Christian Roman Empire. In some parts of northern Africa under Roman rule, Christianity flourished. Alexandria and Carthage were both important centers of Christianity.

Some two hundred years later, Islam began with Mohammad (570–632), who lived both in Mecca and Medina, cities in what today is Saudi Arabia. During the last ten years of Mohammad's life, the Muslim religion spread quickly in the Arabian Peninsula, which today consists of Saudi Arabia, Yemen, United Arab Emirates, Oman, and Qatar.

As I said earlier, I was struck by the maps in my textbook. First, as just described, there was the map of the Roman Empire, which encompassed the entire Mediterranean and was Christian. Just a few chapters later, a map of the same area showed the results of Muslim expansion. By AD 750, just 118 years after the death of Mohammad, the Islamic expansion stretched from Spain and Portugal in the west, across northern Africa, and throughout the Middle East as far as some western parts of India. In this very short time span, Christianity almost disappeared from vast areas, both in the Middle East and in northern Africa.

Depending on who is telling the story, this rapid change took place because of military conquest, economic reasons, or religious conversion. There is some truth to each of these reasons. It is true that a wave of military conquests took place. Justo Gonzales puts it this way:

> Out of Arabia, a forgotten corner of the world that had been generally ignored by both the Roman and the Persian empires, a tidal wave of conquest arose that threatened to engulf the world. In a few years, the Persian Empire had vanished, and many of

the ancient Roman territories were in Arab
hands. The driving force behind this human
avalanche was Mohammed.[6]

The conquests were of a military nature. Unlike many
conquerors of the past, the government did not force the
Muslim religion on the inhabitants of the land. Christians
and Jews living in these regions were considered by
Muslims to be "people of the book," and their religious
rights were respected, at least to a certain extent. The
Qur'an states "There is no compulsion in religion."[7] Except
when there was. The Qur'an also says, "Fight those of
the People of the Book who do not [truly] believe in God
and the Last Days, who do not forbid what God and His
Messenger have forbidden, who do not obey the rule of
justice, until they pay the tax and agree to submit."[8]

Non-Muslims were required to pay a poll or head tax
(*jizra*).[9] This, of course, was considerably more humane
than some of the treatment Christians had suffered
under the Roman Empire. While one can imagine that
the poll tax might have influenced many people to convert
to Islam, scholars have debated this point. Although we
can speculate based on historical facts, we can't always
know exactly what motivated people in the past to make
the decisions they made. Was it fear? Was it that the
Muslim religion appealed to them? Were they compelled
by military force? Was religion simply so unimportant to
them that they were easily convinced to adhere to Islam
in order to avoid paying taxes? Or were they so poor that
they were forced to give in and convert to Islam in order
to survive?

If you decide to research Islamic expansion, you will easily discover that there are widely diverging explanations as to exactly how Islam was able to spread so quickly. Some will paint Muhammad and his followers as warriors who fought ferociously and swiftly conquered vast lands. Others will point to the draw of the Muslim religion, which caused so many people to willingly convert to Islam. Be sure to read more than one side of this discussion because there is certainly some truth in each of these divergent explanations.

At any rate, Islam spread very quickly. First in the Middle East, where the cities of Damascus fell in 635, Antioch in 637, and Jerusalem in 638. Then, from 640–712, Islam spread across northern Africa and into most of modern-day Spain and Portugal. Europeans were afraid that, from Spain, Islam would spread over the Pyrenees Mountains into Western Europe. Muslim invaders did in fact enter what is today the country of France, but in AD 732, Charles Martel defeated the Muslims at the Battle of Tours. This marked the end of the first wave of Muslim expansion.[10]

Later, Europe sought to turn back Islam in the east with what came to be known as the Crusades. The history of the Crusades is complex and has been interpreted by historians in very different ways. Basically, the purpose of the Crusades was to reclaim the Holy Land from the Muslims. If you consider the rapid expansion of Islam throughout North Africa and the Middle East, you can easily imagine why Europeans felt threatened. With the rise of Islam came the belief that Christians had a religious obligation to take up the cross "in order to recapture the

Holy Land—and the land in which Jesus had lived and taught—from the infidel Muslim, in order to facilitate or expedite the return of Christ.[11]

The Crusades had many negative results in relationships between Europe and the Middle East. Hugh Goddard summarizes the legacy of the Crusades:

> Among Muslims, they left a lasting suspicion of Western Christians; they helped to provoke the revival of Muslim expansion; they produced among Muslims greater emphasis on Jerusalem as the third Holy Place of Islam; the Crusades contributed to a worsening of the position of Christians under Muslim rule; they furthered the involvement of the Western Church in the Middle East; and they contributed to the development of contacts between the Muslim world and Western Europe.[12]

Why does any of this matter to us today? One could certainly argue that, from its inception, Islam has been not just a religion but a political movement that seeks to conquer other nations. Of course, the same argument could be made concerning Christianity, although unlike Mohammad, who led military conquests, Jesus certainly was not a warrior. There have been, however, military conquests, such as the Crusades, that were fought in the name of Christianity.

Is there anything we can learn from this? Perhaps. To begin, we who live in the United States of America—as well as those in other nations where freedom of religion is a cherished value—can be very thankful. Throughout human history, the freedom to worship as one chooses has not been a given. Religious freedom is a gift we should never take for granted.

But perhaps you are thinking that Islam is an evil religion and Muslims want to destroy us! We must get rid of them! I will not argue with the fact that heinous acts have been done in the name of Islam. However, I think we need to be careful about calling Islam evil. In the next chapter, we will look at Islamic extremism, which certainly has done evil things and continues to be a threat in our world today. I will not argue in favor of simply saying that all Muslims are harmless and peace loving. The Bible tells us that, when Jesus sent out the twelve disciples, he told them, "I am sending you out like sheep among wolves. Therefore be as shrewd as snakes and as innocent as doves" (Matthew 10:16). That strikes me as very good advice for us today. We can be innocent in our attitudes toward all people, but we also need to be shrewd. Naïveté can seem like a good thing, but it can also be dangerous.

Chapter 6

Islamic Extremism

On September 11, 2001, we literally woke up to the news of the attack on the Twin Towers. But we also woke up intellectually to the fact that things are not right in our world, and we woke up emotionally to the realization that places we assumed were safe might not be. Certainly, there had been random hijackings and some car bombs in Europe, but the 9/11 attacks were something inconceivable in the minds of almost every American.

At the time of the 9/11 attacks, I knew very little about Islamic extremism. I remember seeing pictures of the Ayatollah Khomeini, and later, Osama bin Laden, and hearing about Islamic acts of terror, but I had no idea that what was happening somewhere in the Middle East could have an impact on me. I now know that there were, in fact, those who saw a major attack coming and realized that there were Islamacists who were planning a major terrorist attack on the United States. Both the CIA and the FBI were trying to find out what was going on. Still, even they were caught off guard.[13] How could we comprehend the fact that people in caves halfway around the world were plotting to destroy us? And further, how could we have understood that they had the capability of carrying out significant attacks on American soil? Even more, how could we imagine that these extremists would have so many followers?

Today, it is impossible not to be aware of Islamic terrorism because acts of terrorism are rampant in the Middle East and parts of Africa, and they frequently arise in the United States and Europe. Why is this? What do terrorists want? A simple answer would be that these acts are caused by extremists who want to terrify with the ultimate goal of destroying Western civilization. But why?

Some will point to issues concerning Western need for oil in the Middle East, but while this is a contributing factor, I would argue that it is not the central issue.

Rather, the underlying philosophical issue of Islamic terrorism is the belief that in Muslim communities and nations, the old ways have been lost, and modernity, and in particular the West, is responsible for this loss. Whether or not it ever was, there is a belief that the Islamic world was once ruled by the religion of Islam. The law of the land was Sharia law, which is based on the Qur'an and the Hadith. Men ruled according to these laws and customs, and women, for the most part, stayed at home and out of sight, where they belonged. Every part of life was ruled by the religion of Islam: the food you ate, the prayers you recited five times each day, the way business was conducted, and the way marriages were arranged.

This is absolutely not to say that every Muslim who longs for the old ways is inclined toward extremism. It is one thing to long for a world where things are as they once were, and it is quite another thing to be willing to commit acts of terrorism in order to make your wish come true.

Islamacists want their world to be the way, in their minds, it once was. They see Western civilization as an enormous influence on their world and the major factor contributing to the deterioration of Muslim values. If you grew up in a very conservative family and religious community, you might be able to identify with and at least partially understand this desire for the things of the past. If you accepted the ways of your family and their religion, and you still want to live your life according to those values, you might be very unhappy with modernity. On the other hand, if you grew up and rejected your family's values, you might resent what you see as the backward ways of the past. Magnify these cultural clashes, and it gives you some understanding of the ideological conflict that has been going on for quite some time in predominantly Muslim countries.

When we think about Islamic terrorism, we wrestle with several questions: Why do they hate us? Who are the ones we need to worry about? Who are these terrorists? Do all Muslims hate us—whether they admit it or not? How can we know who we can trust? Should we be afraid of Muslims?

I have sat with enough Muslims in casual settings and in forums, and traveled in enough predominantly Muslim countries that I can say with complete confidence that not all Muslims hate us. I am absolutely certain that not all Muslims are hateful toward Westerners, Americans, or Christians. In fact, I think it would be very safe to say that *most* Muslims do not hate us. On the other hand, I will readily admit that we have seen cases in the United States where a seemingly peaceful person who is a Muslim has suddenly perpetrated an act of terrorist violence. It is also true, however, that we have seen cases where a seemingly peaceful person who is not a Muslim has perpetrated an act of terrorist violence.

If you look up statistics on acts of terrorism on American soil throughout our history, you will see that the number of those perpetrated by Muslims are actually in the minority. The difference is that, first, the attacks of September 11, 2001, had such horrendous consequences in terms of human lives that they will never be forgotten. Second, the weapons used in terrorist acts, including automatic rifles, bombs, and aircraft, have become increasingly capable of causing more deaths. Third, acts involving Muslims tend to be more prevalent in recent history.[14]

Christians are called to love their neighbors—and even to love their enemies. I do not believe this means we are to be naïve. We need to be aware of what is going on in our world. As individuals and as a nation, we need to take precautions in order to stay safe. On the other hand, we must never fall into the trap of being afraid of everything and everyone. Fear can be as dangerous as naïveté.

We can be grateful that our country has in place many safeguards that prevent most of those people who wish to harm us from even entering our country. Does this always work? Of course not. The truth is that nothing can ever be done anywhere that can protect all people from any possible threats to their safety. You could live next to the same neighbor for decades and think you know the person, and one day he or she could purchase an automatic weapon and decide to go outside and shoot all the children in your neighborhood. Thankfully, such things rarely happen, but we have to admit that such things occasionally do happen.

Terrorism is difficult to understand. The neighbor who suddenly becomes violent and begins shooting is probably either extremely hateful or mentally ill—and probably both. Generally, this is not the case with Islamic terrorists.

Islamic extremists, some of whom are terrorists, are usually politically and ideologically motivated. It is true they harbor a kind of hatred toward those who think differently than they do, but their primary motivation is societal change. And while I am sometimes tempted to call acts of terrorism insane, the majority of Islamic extremists are quite sane.

It might surprise you to know that many Islamic terrorists have wives and children. They have families they love. Many of them are well educated.

Islamic extremists believe there is something very wrong with the world, and their desire is to purify the world in accordance with their religion. They see themselves as losing the battle against modernity. Bruce Hoffman, professor at Georgetown University writes, "Cast perpetually on the defensive and forced to take up arms to protect themselves and their real or imagined constituents only, terrorists perceive themselves as reluctant warriors, driven by desperation—and lacking any viable alternative—to violence against a repressive state, a predatory rival ethnic or nationalist group, or an unresponsive international order."[15]

Islamists long for a return to the caliphate. The caliphate is a form of government that is ruled by a caliph, who is the religious leader. In the caliphate, the government rules according to Sharia law, which is based on the Qur'an and other Muslim teachings. Such a government is religious rather than secular. Throughout history, there have been many theocracies or nations ruled by religious leaders according to religious laws. Today, such governments are in the minority. The only Christian state is Vatican City, and the only Muslim nations that are actual Islamic states are Afghanistan, Iran, Mauritania, Saudi Arabia, Sudan, and Yemen.[16]

Even if we understand this longing for the old ways of Islam, it is challenging for most Westerners to comprehend Islamic extremism. One thing that might be helpful is to look at Sayyid Qutb, an Islamic thinker and writer who was highly influential in shaping the thinking of Islamic extremists.

Sayyid Qutb (1906–1966) "was an Egyptian author, educator, Islamic theorist, poet, and the leading member of the Egyptian Muslim Brotherhood in the 1950s and 1960s. In 1966 he was convicted of plotting the assassination of Egyptian president Gamal Abdel Nasser and was executed by hanging."[17]

He wrote extensively, explaining the nature of Islam. In *The Sayyid Qutb Reader,* a collection of his writings, Qutb writes:

> Islam is a declaration of the freedom of man from servitude to other men. Thus it strives from the beginning to abolish all

those systems and governments which are
based on the rule of man over men. ... When
Islam releases people from this political
pressure and presents to them its spiritual
message ... it gives them complete freedom
to accept or not to accept its beliefs.[18]

Qutb is arguing that human governments are by nature
oppressive, but under Islam, people are free. He reiterates
the assertion in the Qur'an that people are given the
freedom to accept Islam or not. According to the Qur'an,
sura 2, verse 256, "There is no compulsion in religion."
The logic Qutb is presenting is that once people have been
freed from their oppressive non-Muslim governments or
belief systems, they will be free to accept Islam.

In the following excerpt, Qutb discusses *jihad*. *Jihad* is
the Arabic word which is translated *struggle* or *exertion*
and can refer to the personal struggle to live a righteous
life and also to the efforts made to defend Islam. Qutb
writes,

The *jihad* of Islam is to secure complete
freedom for every man throughout the world
by releasing him from servitude to other
human beings so that he may serve his God,
Who is One and Who has no associates.
This is in itself a sufficient reason for *jihad*.[19]

Qutb's argument here is that jihad is justified because
it frees people from the systems that keep them from
serving God (Allah). To be fair, we must acknowledge that

others have waged war in the name of their religions, and Christianity is no exception.

In one sense, most religious people believe they have found the best way, and it is not surprising that they would want to influence others on behalf of their religion. Qutb expresses his vision for change in the world in this way:

> Islam is a revolutionary concept and a way of life, which seeks to change the prevalent social order and remould it according to its own vision. ... *Jihad* signifies that revolutionary struggle involving the utmost use of resource is that the Islamic party mobilizes in the service of its cause ... *jihad* ... stands for exerting one's utmost endeavor to promote a cause.[20]

Qutb's vision is to change the world.

> Islamic *jihad* seeks to replace the dominance of non-Islamic systems. This revolution is not territorial but international. ... It is innate in its nature to embrace the whole world, for the truth refuses to be confined to geography. ... No segment of humanity should be barred of its compassion. Whenever humans are oppressed, it must come to their rescue.[21]

Qutb appears to be arguing that war of any sort is justifiable until the entire world is freed from all human governments. Only then will all people be free to accept the teachings of Islam. One might ask, however, how, once all governments have been destroyed, those who do not accept Islam will be dealt with. We might also point out that, throughout history, wars in the name of religion have never been successful in changing people's hearts.

Qutb admits this is a problem. During the Prophet's lifetime, he writes,

> it was practically demonstrated that it was impossible to achieve coexistence between two diametrically opposed ways of life with such deep-rooted and fundamental differences that affect every detail of concepts, beliefs, moral values, social behaviour, as well as social, economic and political structures. We have one way of life based entirely on submission of all mankind to God alone who has no partners, and another that makes people submit to other human beings and false deities. The two are bound to be in conflict at every step and in every aspect of life.[22]

Qutb writes that "Christianity grew up in the shadow of the Roman Empire, in a period when Judaism was suffering an eclipse, when it had become a system of rigid and lifeless ritual, an empty and unspiritual sham. ... Christ (upon who be peace) came only to preach spiritual purity, mercy, kindness ..."

Qutb goes on to explain that the religion of Christianity was only between a man and his God "since Christianity grew up in the embrace of the Roman Empire, and since it was a reaction against Judaism."[23] He goes on to explain this as the reason why Christianity did not include a system of government (as Islam does). Unlike Christianity, Islam "grew up in an independent country owing allegiance to no empire. ... It had to join together the world and the faith by its exhortations and laws. So Islam chose to unite earth and heaven in a single system, present both in the heart of the individual and the actuality of society ..."[24]

Reading Qutb, it is apparent that he sincerely believes that Islamic jihad is a gift that has the capacity of saving the world from its current malaise.

> It may well become apparent to us if we look back on our heritage that we have something to give to this unhappy, perplexed, and weary world, something which it has lost in the present material and unspiritual frame of mind that led to two world wars within a quarter of a century; something which the world is continually trampling under foot in its progress towards a third war, which all the present portents indicate will end in complete ruin.[25]

Qutb's goal is to save the world, and he sees Islamic *jihad* as the solution.

Keeping track of Islamic extremists is difficult. They don't necessarily advertise themselves to the world and announce their intentions. To read more about terrorist groups, an excellent resource is the US State Department website, http://www.state.gov. On that website, search for "Foreign Terrorist Organizations."

Chapter 7

Religious Hatred and Violence

The earliest recorded incident of religious hatred and violence, as far as I know, is the story in chapter four of Genesis, the first book of the Bible. Cain and Abel, the sons of Adam and Eve, brought sacrifices before God.

> Now Abel kept flocks, and Cain worked the soil. In the course of time Cain brought some of the fruits of the soil as an offering to the Lord. But Abel brought fat portions from some of the firstborn of his flock. The Lord looked with favor on Abel and his offering, but on Cain and his offering he did not look with favor. So Cain was very angry, and his face was downcast. (Genesis 4:2–5)

In his anger, Cain led his brother out to a field, attacked him, and killed him. Then, the Lord said to Cain, "Where is your brother?" God's question to Cain seems reminiscent of the question God asked Cain's father, Adam, in the previous chapter. "Then the man and his wife heard the sound of the Lord God as he was walking in the garden in the cool of the day, and they hid from the Lord God among the trees of the garden. But the Lord God called to the man, 'Where are you?'" (Genesis 3:8–9).

God's first question, addressed to Adam, who has just sinned and is hiding from God, is "Where are you?" And his second question, addressed to Cain, who has just slain his brother, is "Where is your brother?" Whether you see these stories as actual factual events or as stories that were written to teach us about relationships between God and humans, they are stories that continue to intrigue us and cause us to think because they speak the unvarnished truth concerning human sin. The image of the Garden of Eden, a place God created as a perfect environment for humankind, is something we all long for. When we pause, open our eyes, and breathe in the beauty of our world, we experience a touch of the Garden of Eden, a symbol of God's creation. Yet that garden's pristine beauty was quickly marred by sin. In the same way, when we hear of murders and wars in our world, we mourn the stain of sin in our world.

Cain's anger with his brother, Abel, took place in what should have been a holy moment. It was a moment when they both stopped their work, brought something of their labors, and presented it as a sacrifice before God. Now, if you're like me, you might be asking, "Why didn't God make it more clear to them both in the first place? Why did God wait until Cain did it 'wrong' before looking upon his sacrifice with disfavor?" Having read the commentaries, I have yet to hear an explanation that completely satisfies me. I conclude that this is something I need to accept, trusting that God has ways that are beyond my understanding.

Both God's questions and our questions matter as to how we see people and religions that are different from our own. There is in this story a triangle between God, Cain, and Abel. Cain brings his offering. Abel brings his offering. Both offerings are presented to God. God then responds to each of them. God is satisfied with Abel's offering, but God did not look favorably on Cain's offering.

The Bible doesn't really explain exactly why God is not pleased, but it does tell us how Cain responded. Cain was angry and his face was downcast. Now, at this point, God speaks to Cain, saying, "Why are you angry? Why is your face downcast? If you do what is right, will you not be accepted? But if you do not do what is right, sin is crouching at your door; it desires to have you, but you must master it" (Genesis 4:6–7).

As I understand this, God is telling Cain that he can make some changes in his sacrifice, and he will be accepted. Further, God is warning Cain against taking an action in his anger that he must resist. Thinking again about the triangle represented by Cain, Abel, and God, this shows that God relates both to Cain and to Abel. There is no problem in either of these relationships that cannot be resolved. Abel's sacrifice has been accepted by God. Cain is told by God that if he does what is right, he will also be accepted. The problem comes when Cain turns his anger on his brother. Even though God warns Cain that sin is crouching at his door, Cain acts on his anger against God and his jealous anger against his brother, and he commits the first murder.

This murder is, in essence, over whose religion is best. Further, these stories seem to tell us that right from the very beginning, God seems to favor some religious practices over others. Regardless of preference, God does tell Cain, "If you do what is right, will you not be accepted?" In other words, God is willing to work with Cain. In the God-Cain-Abel triangle, God remains open to both Cain and Abel. It is the side of the triangle between Cain and Abel that is irreparably broken. I wonder if this is not a symbol that represents the religions of our world today. God is God for all religions and all peoples. The dissension arises between people over their religious differences. If we are able to let go of our desire to judge one another and leave the judging to God, perhaps we can get along with each other. Our dissension is a little bit like the classic and eternal question between siblings as to who Mom likes best. God has enough love for all of us, so we don't need to fight over God.

But that has not stopped us from fighting with one another, has it? War in the name of religion starts in the Bible, and it never seems to stop. The Jewish Bible or Hebrew scriptures, which for Christians is the Old Testament, has more battles and wars than I could begin to number. It seems to have been part of the culture from the beginning. I confess I find one verse particularly telling and a little bit humorous because it seems to indicate that war was simply the way of life. It says, "In the spring, at the time when kings go off to war" (2 Samuel 11:1a). Apparently, there's no particular reason for these wars except that the weather is right. Tragically, the rest of the chapter and following tells a very sad story about King David.

We Christians might think all of those wars ended with the coming of Jesus and the beginning of the early church, but not so. At first, there were little disagreements among the Christians. Which widows among the new believers were getting the best treatment: the Grecian Jews or the Hebraic Jews? (Acts 7:1–7). Thankfully, that squabble was apparently settled quickly and easily. Soon, there were disagreements as to how closely the new believers needed to follow the dietary laws of the Jews. Later, there was a disagreement over whether non-Jews converting to Christianity needed to be circumcised. All of these and other issues were within the Christian church in the earliest days of its history.

In the history of the world, many battles have been fought in the name of God, and my guess is that in most, and even perhaps in all of them, God was not pleased. It is way beyond the scope of this book to even begin to name all of the battles that have been fought over the centuries, using religion as at least a partial rationale.

One easy answer would be to conclude that all religions are worthless and dangerous and should be abolished. Many people, in fact, have come to that conclusion. Of course, removing religion from the equation of human affairs would not bring about world peace. However, I believe those of us who call ourselves Christians would do well to pause and think carefully about the wars that have used the name of Christ to bring violence against other nations or people groups.

Under the Nazi regime of Germany during World War II, some six million Jews were murdered. Most of the Germans who carried out these atrocities considered themselves Christians. When we look at this event in hindsight, it seems to be evil beyond belief. Yet it happened. Fine, upstanding Christian citizens of Germany committed horrendous atrocities against their German neighbors who happened to be Jewish.

If I had never read the Bible and started reading it from the beginning, my mouth would drop open when Cain killed his brother. How could he do such a thing? Why would he do such a thing? Why blame Abel? We would do well to remember that, like Cain, we are all capable of sinning. When we fail to love our fellow humans, sin is crouching at our door.

Today, the ravages of man's inhumanity to man in the form of terrorism, war, and genocide come right into our homes on the television screen. At this particular moment in history, I think it would be safe to say that the majority of these incidents involve Islamic terrorists in one form or another. Because of this, it is very easy for us to lump all Muslims together and identify them as "the enemy."

This is, at a minimum, a dangerous oversimplification. There is no question about the fact that we have some very serious issues in our world today, and Islamic terrorism is right up at the top of the list.

How do we who call ourselves Christians approach this situation? I believe the first thing is to seek God's wisdom through our good, old-fashioned, trustworthy method of reading our Bibles and praying. Further, we need to do everything with utmost humility. If we are truly humble, we will be able to admit that we Christians have not always been the innocents in history. We have gotten things horribly wrong in the past, and we may very well get them wrong again, unless we are open to approaching our neighbors as Jesus taught us. Jesus said, "You have heard that it was said, 'Love your neighbor and hate your enemy.' But I tell you: Love your enemies and pray for those who persecute you, that you may be sons of your Father in heaven" (Matthew 5:43–45).

Jesus's words teach us to begin by loving our enemies and praying for them. *Fiddler on the Roof* tells the story of a Jewish village fighting for their own existence under the anti-Jewish pogroms in Russia. In the play, a young man asks the rabbi, "Is there a proper blessing for the tsar?" The rabbi quickly responds, "A blessing for the tsar? Of course! May God bless and keep the tsar … far away from us!" The humor in this exchange is a gentle reminder that we can pray in every circumstance.

We can pray for Islamic extremists: that their hearts will be changed. And, as the rabbi instructs in his blessing for the tsar, we can also pray that they do not harm us. The important thing is that we pray. All of us want peace in our world, beginning in our homes and our communities and extending to our nation and the world.

Perhaps we need to listen to the questions God asked in Genesis. God asked Adam and Eve, "Where are you?" Am I wandering off, doing as I please, as Adam and Eve did in the Garden of Eden? Or am I seeking God's presence in my life. God asked Cain, "Where is your brother?" I wonder if God is asking me how I am treating those who worship God in ways that are different from my own ways. War and violence of any sort are tragic, but war and violence in the name of religion must surely pierce God's own heart.

Chapter 8

Who Ya Gonna Hate?

Most likely, you have sung the Christmas carol, "I Heard the Bells on Christmas Day," with its beautiful, thought-provoking lyrics. The song is a slightly shortened version of the poem by Henry Wadsworth Longfellow, first published in 1866. In most hymnals, the fourth and fifth verses of the poem, which I include below, are omitted. In order to understand Longfellow's poem, it is helpful to know that Longfellow's poem was published shortly after the thirteenth amendment to the Constitution of the United States, prohibiting slavery, was ratified, on December 6, 1865.

I heard the bells on Christmas Day
Their old, familiar carols play,
And wild and sweet
The words repeat
Of peace on earth, good-will to men!

And thought how, as the day had come,
The belfries of all Christendom
Had rolled along
The unbroken song
Of peace on earth, good-will to men!

Till, ringing, singing on its way,
The world revolved from night to day,
A voice, a chime,
A chant sublime
Of peace on earth, good-will to men!

Then from each black, accursed mouth
The cannon thundered in the South,
And with the sound
The carols drowned
Of peace on earth, good-will to men!

It was as if an earthquake rent
The hearth-stones of a continent,
And made forlorn
The households born
Of peace on earth, good-will to men!

And in despair I bowed my head;
"There is no peace on earth," I said:
"For hate is strong,
And mocks the song
Of peace on earth, good-will to men!"

Then pealed the bells more loud and deep:
"God is not dead; nor doth he sleep!
The Wrong shall fail,
The Right prevail,
With peace on earth, good-will to men!"[26]

The poem in its entirety tells us that Longfellow was writing in response to the shame of slavery, which had gone on for so long in America. Even though I had never read the verses that refer to slavery, I have always sung this song with full awareness that hate is indeed strong in our world. It always touches me to be able to admit to the despair I often feel when I realize that "hate is strong, and mocks the song of peace on earth, good-will to men." Yet my heart rejoices as we continue to sing, joyfully affirming that the bells still peal more loud and deep: "God is not dead; nor doth he sleep! The Wrong shall fail, The Right prevail, With peace on earth, good-will to men."

Longfellow's words remind me that I can look squarely into the face of hatred, bow my head in despair, and still affirm that God is not dead; God is not sleeping. There is hope. As Longfellow writes, hate is indeed strong. Although his words were written more than 150 years ago—although slavery was declared illegal more than 150 years ago—racism still lives on. Longfellow understood that abolishing slavery would not abolish hatred. Hatred is alive and well in our world today.

By now, you may be muttering to yourself, "Well, I don't hate anyone." Still, every one of us needs to do some soul-searching from time to time. Have any little seeds of hatred taken root and sprouted in our hearts? Even a little bit of hate is capable of immense destruction.

Hate is, of course, a very strong word, and most of us don't like to think of ourselves as hating anyone. As Christians, we are fully aware of the fact that Jesus calls us to love. Jesus said, "You have heard that it was said, 'Love your neighbor and hate your enemy.' But I tell you: 'Love your enemies and pray for those who persecute you'" (Matthew 5:43–44). First John states, "Anyone who claims to be in the light but hates his brother is still in the darkness" (1 John 2:9) and "If anyone says 'I love God,' yet hates his brother, he is a liar" (1 John 4:20). These are very strong warnings, written to Christians, and none of us wants to admit we are guilty of hatred.

Maybe we could start by talking about the hate we observe in our families, in our communities, in our nation, and in our world. Unless you live in a cave and never come out, you are aware of the enormous amount of hatred in our world. Since we're talking in this book about Muslims, let's be honest: many, many Americans and Europeans harbor a good deal of hate in their hearts toward Muslims. And to be fair, many Muslims hate Americans, Europeans, and others. Right now, in this moment of world history, hatred between Muslims and Christians or Westerners certainly is at the top of the hate list.

But hate doesn't stop there. When Longfellow wrote "Christmas Bells," slavery had ended. But Longfellow knew, and as we know today, ending slavery was not the end of hatred against black people. The ugliness of racism lives on. Every time I think that we as a nation have made progress and racism is no longer much of a problem, an incident in the news reminds me of just how wrong I am. When I listen to the stories my African American friends tell about how they are treated, I am ashamed of my white race.

I grew up singing, "Jesus loves the little children, all the children of the world, red and yellow, black and white, they are precious in his sight, Jesus loves the little children of the world." I understood that meant we were to love everyone, just as Jesus does, regardless of skin color. I assumed that I was completely against racism of every sort.

However, I admit that I grew up in a white bubble. I grew up in Seattle, and at that time, it was so racially segregated that I rarely even saw a person of color. As a child, the only time I remember seeing black people was when we were downtown and passed a certain bus stop where they all stood. Their bus went a different direction than my bus. My class pictures from elementary school show only white children. There was one Jewish girl in my class in sixth grade, and she was one of my friends. My high school had two black students, one of whom was an exchange student from Africa. We were not prejudiced, of course. We were just all white. But when a white girl moved to our community from Alabama, we hated her because she was from the South. We mercilessly blamed her for the entire history of slavery and the Civil War. In fact, one of my history teachers spoke so cruelly to her in class about Southern history that I ended up being on her side. But of course, I didn't actually tell her that. I wish I could go back and apologize, Sally.

We Seattleites were proud not to be like those terrible racists in the South. Much later, I learned that some of our history proved we were not so innocent. I was never told the stories of Japanese Americans in our city having been forced to leave their homes and live in internment camps during World War II. It was only a couple of years ago that I learned of our shameful treatment of Chinese immigrants. In the mid 1800s, many Chinese people were brought to the United States to build our railroads. When the work was finished, some of them ended up in Tacoma, Washington, where they built a small settlement on the banks of Puget Sound. During the economic slump that began in 1873, Washingtonians began to blame the Chinese for their problems. On November 7, 1885, the entire Chinese population of the little settlement—from children to old people—was marched to the railroad station and forced to leave. The next day, their homes were burned to the ground.[27] Today, you can visit Chinese Reconciliation Park on that same spot and read about this sad and shameful event in our history.

We also learned very little in school about how we had displaced Native Americans. Once again, in my white bubble world, I knew so little. I have one childhood memory that many years later I realized was formative in my views toward Native Americans. I was walking with my parents in the small town where they grew up, and I saw a person sitting on the sidewalk, hunched over against a building. I had never seen someone sleeping on the sidewalk, and I was very troubled. My dad said to me, "Oh, that's just an old drunk Indian. It's nothing you need to worry about." I must have persisted, because he then explained, "He'll be okay. One of his people will come along and drag him home." I realize now that this encounter colored my assumptions concerning Native Americans. It taught me that they have drinking problems and that their problems are not our problems. Further, because I grew up in a family where consuming alcohol was considered sinful, I probably also assumed these people were morally inferior. Many years later, I realized I needed to think about how those childhood impressions had allowed me to stereotype an entire people group, putting them neatly into a box that need not concern me. I suppose it is true that I didn't hate them, but I certainly did not love them.

With respect to religion, I grew up being taught that Christianity was the only true religion—and that all other religions were false. In particular, the Christianity I was taught was Protestant and Evangelical. I was taught that, as a Christian, my duty was to preach the gospel to all people. Since I was a rather shy child, this seemed like a difficult responsibility. I liked the words of the Great Commission of Jesus: "Go and make disciples of all nations, baptizing them in the name of the Father and of the Son and of the Holy Spirit, and teaching them to obey everything I have commanded you. And surely I am with you always, to the very end of the age" (Matthew 28:19–20). The people I admired most of all as child were missionaries. I thought God might want me to be a missionary, but I was afraid I would end up having to go somewhere with lots of snakes. Since I'm afraid of snakes, I hoped not.

We never were taught to hate people who were not Christians. Mostly, we learned to feel sorry for them.

Cathy Sovold Johnson

However, if we look at people with pity because they are not like us, is that not at least a form of prejudice?

People are hated because of race, religion, ethnicity, economic standing, political persuasion, sexual identity, and nationality—the list goes on. It seems that some of these hatreds lie dormant at times, and then something happens that causes hatred to bubble to the surface. Often, the thing that incites a new wave of hatred has to do with the economy. Economic turmoil incites people to look around for someone to blame, and all of their prejudices start to erupt.

An example of this in recent history is the Holocaust, the horrendous treatment of Jews under Hitler. Anti-Semitism still, to this day, exists among Christians. Negative attitudes toward Jews are deeply entrenched in the Christian church. The hatred toward Jews so permeated the teachings of the Christian Church that it was possible for millions of Germans to support and willingly participate in the atrocities of the Holocaust. Martin Luther is well respected for his contributions to the Protestant Reformation, but his attitudes toward Jews are despicable. In spite of his brilliant mind and contributions to theological discourse, he was still blind to the anti-Semitism of his culture.

It has been all too easy for we Christians to dismiss or try to bury the anti-Semitism of Luther, as well as other church leaders. However, at the International Congress for Luther Research in 1971, the president stated:

> I have read—and indeed I have sometimes
> repeated—most of the conventional defenses

of Luther's harsh language about the Jews. ...
I cannot escape the conviction that the time
has come for those who study Luther and
admire him to acknowledge ... that on this
issue Luther's thought and language are
simply beyond defense.[28]

If a man as devout, learned, and brilliant as Luther
could be so very wrong in his view of Jews, most likely
greatly impacted by his own cultural upbringing, all of us
need to admit that we may very well have some glaring
blind spots in our own attitudes toward others.

Lest we blame the Holocaust solely on the German
Lutherans, we need to add that many German Catholics
were complicit as well. Rudolf Hoess, the commandant of
Auschwitz, was raised a devout Catholic. In his postwar
autobiography, Hoess stated: "I personally arranged on
orders received from Himmler in May 1941 the gassing
of two million persons between June–July 1941 and
the end of 1943."[29] Franklin Littell assesses, "Nothing
Hoess was taught in a Christian home or in the church ...
instructed him as to the time and place to say no to wicked
commands."[30]

When we look back at these and other failures of the
church in its response to racism and anti-Semitism, it
feels very sad. While we know there were people who
were exceptions, it feels sad to realize how many fine,
upstanding Christians could have been so wrong in their
treatment of people they saw as different. Thinking about
this reality of our past is a warning to us. It demonstrates
the fact that we can be shortsighted. All of us are capable

of being swayed by hateful rhetoric. All of us are capable of allowing hate to color our hearts.

Muslims are easy to hate for several reasons. First, they often look different than most of us. Most of them come from parts of the world we have never visited. The women distinguish themselves by covering their heads with scarves. Their religion is different than ours. Many of them have cultural practices that are foreign to us. All that before we even start to talk about the centuries of wars between Muslim nations and the West. Add to that the more modern events of Islamic terrorism. What's more, there are so many of them in the world today that they may even threaten our existence!

Can you blame us for having some problems loving our Muslim neighbors? When you think about all of the differences among people that form the basis of our prejudices, fear is almost always part of the equation: fear that we somehow will be displaced by these other people, fear that they will somehow challenge our rights to be who we thought we were in the place we want to be, and fear that there's not enough room in the world for all of us with all of our differences.

People are hated for so many reasons—skin color, religion, ethnicity, sexual orientation, and political persuasion. The list goes on and on. Most of the time, wrapped up in that hate is a great deal of fear of the other. What or who are you afraid of? Whose very existence on this planet—and particularly in your neighborhood—challenges your rights? Who are you gonna hate?

Chapter 9

Allah

Christians often wonder, "Who is Allah?" If Muslims worship Allah, is Allah a different god from our God? The word *Allah* is the Arabic word for *God*. While it is true that Muslims and Christians have many differences in how they view Allah or God, that does not change the nature of Allah or God. Just as Cain and Abel chose to worship God in different ways by offering different sacrifices in the Genesis account, Christians, Jews, and Muslims also understand and worship God in different ways. Regardless of our different concepts of God and regardless of our relationship to God, God is God. Whether you speak Arabic and the word you use for God is Allah, or you speak English and the word you use for God is God, God is God. Not every person who worships God or Allah has the same understanding of who God or Allah is.

A number of years ago, when I was just beginning to learn about Islam, I visited a mosque during their Friday afternoon prayer service. This was a rather small and simple mosque. They graciously offered me a seat in the back of the room, from which to observe. I watched and listened as they went about their prayers in Arabic, standing, sitting, and kneeling. Of course, I did not understand what was being said. Somewhat bored, I quietly studied the room, the patterns on the wall, and the plaques in Arabic script.

Suddenly, I felt an overwhelming presence of the Holy Spirit. Completely surprised, I said (not audibly) to God, "What are you doing here?"

Immediately, the response came, again not audibly, "Haven't you always believed I am everywhere present?"

"Of course," I responded. "Of course you are here, God. I do believe that you are everywhere present."

Afterward, I apologized to God for my knee-jerk prayer, "What are you doing here?" as it seemed a bit irreverent. But God clearly understood and honored me and answered me in that moment. Now that I think about it, maybe God likes our knee-jerk prayers better than our carefully thought-out, sometimes contrived prayers—at least some of the time.

For me, this was truly a holy moment. Ever since that brief little experience, I have been confident that God is truly with me when I am interacting with people of different religions. I don't need to be afraid because God is there with me.

The Arabic word for God, Allah, is the word that Arabic-speaking Christians use to refer to their Christian God. When Mohammad first began to teach and preach, his primary call to the people was to stop worshipping their many pagan gods and to worship the one true Allah. One of the shortest surahs of the Qur'an expresses the oneness and mercy of Allah: "In the name of God, the

Lord of Mercy, the Giver of Mercy. Say, 'He is God the One, God the eternal. He begot no one nor was He begotten. No one is comparable to him'" (surah 112:1–4).

As this Surah demonstrates, Jews, Christians, and Muslims have many points of agreement with respect to God/Allah. We all agree that God is one, God is eternal, and God is merciful.

As a Christian, I would also say that Mohammad had some very different ideas about God than the Bible teaches, and I would have plenty of theological differences with him. However, that does not mean that he does not worship the same God we Christians worship. Our understanding of God is different, but God is the same. That's because God is God, and God far transcends all of our human understandings—even yours and mine!

Jews, Christians, and Muslims are all considered to be the Abrahamic faiths because all of us trace our lineage back to Abraham: Jews and Christians through his son, Isaac, and Muslims through his son, Ishmael. We don't all think alike or pray alike, but we confess that we do have common roots. And we all believe in one God.

Of the Abrahamic faiths, Judaism is the oldest religion, going back to Abraham and Moses. The Jewish or Hebrew scriptures are what Christians know as the Old Testament of the Bible, originally written in Hebrew. The Torah, also known as the Law, consists of the first five books (Genesis, Exodus, Leviticus, Numbers, and Deuteronomy) and forms the central teachings of Judaism. It was into a Jewish family that Jesus was born.

Christianity is the second oldest of the Abrahamic religions, dating itself to the life of Jesus Christ, the Son of God. Christians include the Hebrew scriptures, referred to as the Old Testament, and add to it the New Testament, which was originally written in Greek. The Christian Bible includes the Hebrew scriptures and the New Testament.

Islam, which began with the teachings of Mohammad, who lived from AD 570–632, is the youngest of these three religions. Like Jews and Christians, Muslims trace their roots back to Abraham, through his first son, Ishmael, who was born to the slave woman, Hagar. When Mohammad began to preach, he called on the people to stop worshipping idols and return to worshipping the one true God, who in their Arabic language was named Allah. In one sense, this was a call to return to the God of Abraham.

Muslims have their own scriptures, the Qur'an, a recording of the teachings of Mohammad, originally written in Arabic. The Qur'an has numerous references to people in the Bible, both Old and New Testaments, but whenever these accounts appear in the Qur'an, they tend to differ somewhat from the biblical accounts. I have read these accounts in the Qur'an, and my assumption is that Mohammad's understanding of the Bible came from oral tradition. These differences are not surprising because, in the oral retelling of stories, there are always changes as the account goes from one storyteller to the next.

As a result of their beginnings, Judaism, Christianity, and Islam have similarities and differences. From my Christian viewpoint, we all worship one God. However, Jews, Christians, and Muslims look at one another and disagree on many very basic issues. Both Jews and Muslims see Christians as wrong in our declaration that

Jesus is the Son of God. Christians disagree with both Jews and Muslims and say they are missing the most central tenet of our faith, which is Jesus's message of salvation through his death and resurrection.

Christians also have been guilty of accusing the Jews of killing Jesus, which is an unreasonable accusation for two reasons. First, while the Jewish leaders were, for the most part, united in wanting to kill Jesus, they in no way represented all of the Jews. Quite a few Jews, in fact, were followers of Jesus. Second, the Roman government actually carried out the crucifixion of Jesus, and they could have stopped it if they had chosen to do so. Third, the idea of accusing anyone of killing Jesus is a misunderstanding of Jesus's purpose, part of which was his crucifixion (see John 3:14; 8:28; 12:32–34).

Theologically, Jews and Muslims disagree with Christians over the deity of Jesus. During Jesus's lifetime and after his death, many Jews became Christians, accepting Jesus as their Lord and Savior. Those Jews who did not accept Jesus continued in their Jewish faith. Jews and Christians today read the same words from the Hebrew scriptures, which Christians call the Old Testament. Christians include the Old Testament in their Bible but place great emphasis on the New Testament because it includes the teachings of Jesus, the history and writings of the early church, and the message of salvation through Jesus Christ.

Muslims include in the Qur'an numerous references to people recorded in the Bible, both Old and New Testament. Muslims see Jesus as a true prophet, but they do not believe in his virgin birth—and they do not believe Jesus is the Son of God. Muslims do not believe in the deity of Jesus. Concerning Jesus, the Qur'an says,

> People of the Book, do not go to excess in your religion, and do not say anything about God except the truth: the Messiah, Jesus, son of Mary, was nothing more than a messenger of God, His word, directed to Mary, a spirit from Him. So believe in God and His messengers and do not speak of a "Trinity"—stop [this], that is better for you— God is only one God, He is far above having a son. ... The Messiah would never disdain to be a servant of God. (Qur'an 4:171–172)

Muslims do not believe Jesus was actually crucified. They believe that he only *seemed* to be crucified:

> They did not kill him, nor did they crucify him, though it was made to appear like that to them; those that disagreed about him are full of doubt, with no knowledge to follow, only supposition: they certainly did not kill him—God raised him up to Himself. God is almighty and wise. (Qur'an 4:157)

Muslims see the deity of Jesus as an affront to the oneness of God. They interpret the Christian belief in the Trinity as meaning that Christians have three gods, which would be a form of idolatry. This is actually not surprising. In the first few centuries of Christianity, there were deep disagreements among Christian church leaders and theologians concerning the deity of Jesus and the nature of the Trinity.

To a Jew, a Christian or a Muslim who takes his or her faith seriously, these very basic understandings of God/Allah are radically different. I am in no way arguing in favor of syncretism, where we would say that our differences are inconsequential and it's more important to get along with each other than it is to hold onto our own beliefs. I have Jewish and Muslim friends who would be equally opposed to syncretism. They hold their beliefs as closely as I do mine.

On the other hand, I believe we can learn to appreciate and love one another—whether or not we ever agree in our religions. I believe the only way to approach others, particularly those who have significantly different viewpoints than our own, is with respect, humility, and love.

Chapter 10

Abraham

When I was growing up, we often had Sunday school lessons about "Bible heroes." We learned about these powerful, mostly Old Testament, mostly male historical figures who were brave and strong for God.

As I grew older and read the entire Bible for myself, I learned that the stories we were told as children left out a whole lot about these heroes. I'm not arguing that the sometimes-lurid details of these "heroes" should be told to children, but the reality is—other than Jesus—most of our biblical and modern-day heroes have a few flaws.

Abraham was no exception. Because Muslims sometimes refer to Jews, Christians, and Muslims as the Abrahamic faiths, the stories of Abraham and his family are important to understanding the roots of all three religions. The Bible teaches us that Abraham was a man of faith who believed and obeyed God. When first called by God, his name was Abram.

> The Lord had said to Abram, "Leave your country, your people and your father's

household and go to the land I will show
you. I will make you into a great nation
and I will bless you; I will make your name
great, and you will be a blessing. I will bless
those who bless you and whoever curses you
I will curse; and all peoples on earth will be
blessed through you." (Genesis 12:1–3)

Abram believed God and obeyed, but if you read the
details of the story, he did some things that we might
question. When traveling in a foreign country, he lied,
passing his wife, Sarah, off as his sister, in order to save
his own neck. God promised Abraham that he would be
the father of a great nation. Many years later, when he
and Sarah became frustrated over the fact that she was
still childless, they took things in their own hands. At
Sarah's suggestion, Abraham took Sarah's slave woman,
Hagar, and she gave birth to a son, Ishmael. There are
two problems we as readers of the Bible have with this
story. First is the fact that Abraham was a slave owner.
Second, because of his lack of faith in God's promise and
unwillingness to wait for God's timing, Abraham slept
with Hagar, his wife's servant. When Hagar became
pregnant, Sarai began to mistreat her, and Hagar ran away.
When she ran away, the angel of the Lord found her and
promised her that she would have many descendants—too
numerous to count.

The angel of the Lord also said to her: "You
are now with child and you will have a son.
You shall name him Ishmael, for the Lord

has heard of your misery. He will be a wild
donkey of a man; his hand will be against
everyone and everyone's hand against him,
and he will live in hostility toward all his
brothers" (Genesis 16:11–12)

Hagar returned to Abraham's household, and she gave
birth to Ishmael, Abraham's firstborn son. After the birth
of Ishmael, God again appeared to Abraham, promising
him that Sarah would bear a son. Since so much time
had passed without a child and since he and Sarah were
growing old, Abraham argued with God:

> Abraham fell facedown; he laughed and said
> to himself, "Will a son be born to a man a
> hundred years old? Will Sarah bear a child
> at the age of ninety?" And Abraham said to
> God, "If only Ishmael might live under your
> blessing!" Then God said, "Yes, but your
> wife Sarah will bear you a son, and you will
> call him Isaac. I will establish my covenant
> with him as an everlasting covenant for his
> descendants after him. And as for Ishmael,
> I have heard you: I will surely bless him;
> I will make him fruitful and will greatly
> increase his numbers. He will be the father
> of twelve rulers, and I will make him into
> a great nation. But my covenant I will
> establish with Isaac." (Genesis 17:17–22)

Clearly, God makes a promise concerning the
descendants of Hagar the slave woman's son, Ishmael,

but he says that his covenant will be for the descendants of Sarah's son, Isaac.

The fulfillment of this prophecy concerning Ishmael is alluded to in the account found in Genesis 25, just after the death of Abraham.

> This is the account of Abraham's son Ishmael, whom Sarah's maidservant, Hagar the Egyptian, bore to Abraham. These are the names of the sons of Ishmael, listed in the order of their birth: Nebaioth the firstborn of Ishmael, Kedar, Adbeel, Mibsam, Mishma, Dumah, Massa, Hadad, Tema, Jetur, Naphish and Kedema. These where the sons of Ishmael and these are the names of the twelve tribal rulers according to their settlements and camps. Altogether, Ishmael lived a hundred and thirty-seven years. He breathed his last and died, and he was gathered to his people. His descendants settled in the area from Havilah to Shur, near the border of Egypt, as you go toward Asshur. And they lived in hostility toward all their brothers. (Genesis 25:12–18)

To say the least, this is interesting. The Bible teaches that the Israelites were God's chosen people, but this passage indicates that God also had his hand upon Ishmael and his descendants. God says he will bless Ishmael, but God establishes a covenant with Isaac.

As every Jew and every Christian knows, God finally did bless Abraham and Sarah with a son, Isaac. Abraham was one hundred years old, but Sarah was only a spry, young ninety-year-old. "Sarah said, 'God has brought me laughter, and everyone who hears about this will laugh with me'" (Genesis 21:6).

Unfortunately, the birth of Isaac did not settle the enmity between Sarah and Hagar.

> On the day Isaac was weaned Abraham held a great feast. But Sarah saw that the son that Hagar the Egyptian had borne to Abraham was mocking, and she said to Abraham, "Get rid of that slave woman and her son, for that slave woman's son will never share in the inheritance with my son Isaac." (Genesis 21:8–10)

Distressed, Abraham prays, and he sends Hagar and Ishmael away. Wandering together in the desert, their food and water run out. They sit down and wait to die, but God hears the boy crying and sends an angel. "Lift the boy up and take him by the hand, for I will make him into a great nation" (Genesis 21:18). Then God showed her a well of water, and it tells us that "God was with the boy as he grew up" (Genesis 21:20).

Ishmael shows up once again at the death of his father, Abraham. "His sons Isaac and Ishmael buried him in the cave of Machpelah ... with his wife Sarah" (Genesis 25:9–10).

Jews, Christians, and Muslims all trace their religions back to Abraham, but for Jews and Christians, the lineage continues through Isaac. For Muslims, the lineage continues through Ishmael. The story in Genesis of the sacrifice Abraham almost made of his son, Isaac, is highly disputed by Muslims because they believe this sacrificial event took place with Abraham's first son, Ishmael. One of the reasons Muslims make this claim is that the Genesis account refers to Abraham sacrificing his only son. When he sees that Abraham is willing to obey him and give his son, God interrupts the sacrifice. "'Do not lay a hand on the boy,' he said. 'Do not do anything to him. Now I know that you fear God, because you have not withheld from me your son, your only son'" (Genesis 22:12).

In the Qur'an, Ishmael is the son in this sacrificial event. Abraham says,

> "Lord, grant me a righteous son," so We[31] gave him the good news that he would have a patient son. When the boy was old enough to work with his father, Abraham said, "My son, I have seen myself sacrificing you in a dream. What do you think?" He said, "Father, do as you are commanded, and, God willing, you will find me steadfast." When they had both submitted to God, and he had laid his son down on the side of his face, We called out to him, "Abraham, you have fulfilled the dream." This is how We reward those who do good—it was a test to prove [their true characters]—We ransomed

his son with a momentous sacrifice, and We let him be praised by succeeding generations: "Peace be upon Abraham!" (Qur'an 37:100–109).

Muslims argue that, since Abraham calls the boy his only son, the Bible must be talking about his firstborn son, Ishmael.

The Qur'an also attributes the building of the Ka'ba to Abraham and his son, Ishmael.

> We made the House [the Ka'ba at Mecca] a resort and a sanctuary for people, saying, "Take the spot where Abraham stood as your place of prayer." We commanded Abraham and Ishmael: "Purify My House for those who walk round it, those who stay there, and those who bow and prostrate themselves in worship." (Qur'an 2:125)

According to the Bible, when Abraham died, Isaac and Ishmael went together to bury him. The Bible says,

> Altogether, Abraham lived a hundred and seventy-five years. Then Abraham breathed his last and died at a good old age, an old man and full of years; and was gathered to his people. His sons Isaac and Ishmael buried him in the cave of Machpelah near Mamre, in the field of Ephron son of Zohar the Hittite, the field Abraham had bought from the Hittites. (Genesis 25:7–10)

Often, Muslims who are in favor of positive, peaceful relationships with non-Muslims will point to these passages, emphasizing the fact that Jews, Christians, and Muslims are all Abrahamic faiths.

Chapter 11

Inclusion Versus Exclusion in the Bible and the Qur'an

A very basic part of what defines us as human beings is our religion or lack of religion. Religion defines our understanding of who we are at the very core of our being. It is the way we define ourselves as persons with respect to our understanding of who God is and who we are and how we relate to God and to the world. Even atheists, who believe there is no God, in a sense ascribe to the religion of atheism, which also defines how they see themselves as human beings in a universe that has no God.

Throughout recorded human history, religion has been central in the beliefs of human cultures and groups with respect to how they define both themselves and "the other." "The others" are usually people or groups of people who have a different religion. Although for our purposes, we are limiting ourselves to a discussion of the Abrahamic religions, particularly on Christian-Muslim relationships today, there are many other religions in the world.

Even within each of the Abrahamic religions, there is a broad spectrum of religious practices and beliefs as well as cultural practices. It would be simple if we could say that some in each of these religions are more conservative and some more liberal, but the reality is that this would not begin to adequately describe all of the complexities. Most likely, you have had some personal experiences with this. I remember a time when I met a group of people who had an extremely similar culture and set of beliefs to mine, and it was amazing how quickly I felt so comfortable sitting and chatting with them. It felt as if they were my family. I also remember a time I was with some people who I thought shared my cultural and religious beliefs, but I soon realized it was almost as if we were from different planets. Both of these groups were Christians, but I quickly realized that we simply did not see things in the same way.

These differences and similarities can be very obvious or extremely subtle. They show up in our speech, in our dress, in the foods we eat—and even how we eat those foods—how we spend our time, how we relate to others, and to our politics. All of that is long before we even start talking about God.

The differences concerning how we relate to "the other" can be found in the teachings of all religions, sometimes with welcoming inclusivity and other times with extreme exclusiveness.

When God first appears to Abram (before his name was changed to Abraham) it says:

> The Lord had said to Abram, "Leave your
> country, your people and your father's
> household and go to the land I will show
> you. I will make you into a great nation and I
> will bless you; I will make your name great,
> and you will be a blessing. I will bless those
> who bless you, and whoever curses you I
> will curse; and all peoples on earth will be
> blessed through you." (Genesis 12:1–3)

This seems both exclusive and inclusive. Abram is "the chosen one." That he is the chosen one means all of the others have not been chosen. Yet his purpose in being chosen is so that all peoples on the earth might be blessed. God *also* promises to curse those who curse him. This pattern of the chosen and the "other" continues. Abram, who has been chosen to father a great nation, was childless until he finally became the father of Ishmael, whose mother was not his wife, but Hagar, his wife's slave woman.

Finally, at age one hundred, Abraham (no longer called Abram) has a son by his wife, Sarah, and names him Isaac. When Sarah becomes jealous of the first son, Ishmael, son of Hagar, the slave, Hagar and Ishmael are sent away. It is through Sarah's son, Isaac, that God's promise, or covenant, continues. As the story in the Bible continues, it becomes the story of God's Chosen People, the descendants of Abraham through his son, Isaac. Abraham's first son, Ishmael, is not the chosen one. It is Isaac and his lineage that God chooses.

It is thought that Abraham lived sometime around 2000 BC. As far as the biblical account goes, Ishmael is no longer part of the story of God's covenant with Abraham. However, Genesis tells us that God does provide for Ishmael. Speaking to Abraham,

> God said, "Yes, but your wife Sarah will bear you a son, and you will call him Isaac. I will establish my covenant with him as an everlasting covenant for his descendants after him. And as for Ishmael, I have heard you: I will surely bless him. I will make him fruitful and will greatly increase his numbers. He will be the father of twelve rulers, and I will make him into a great nation." (Genesis 17:19–20)

Even though God has made this promise to Ishmael—and even though it is recorded in the Bible—neither Jews nor Christians over the centuries have upheld Ishmael as part of God's covenant. Is it possible that it was God's intent that Ishmael's exclusion from Abraham's family was for the purpose of bringing a blessing to others? It was a caravan of Ishmaelites, also referred to as Midianites, who bought Joseph from his brothers and took him to Egypt (Genesis 37). Is it possible that God was present in Ishmael's family even though it is not recorded in the Bible?

Some two and a half millennia later, Mohammad, who traced his lineage back to Ishmael, began preaching in Mecca. Mohammad's message to the people was that they must get rid of their idols and return to the worship of the one God, Allah, the God of Abraham. Thus, the third of the Abrahamic religions, Islam, was born.

Islam clearly sees itself as a part of the monotheism of Judaism and Christianity. Mohammad proclaimed, "We[32] sent Noah and Abraham, and gave prophethood and scripture to their offspring. ... We sent other messengers. ... We sent Jesus, son of Mary: We gave him the Gospel and put compassion and mercy into the hearts of his followers ..." (57:26–27). In this surah, the Qur'an argues in favor of inclusion, naming Noah, Abraham, Jesus, and Mary as forerunners of the faith, sent by Allah. This sounds like a plea for an attitude of inclusion. However, a few lines later, it says, "The People of the Book should know that they have no power over any of God's grace and that grace is in the hand of God alone: He gives it to whoever He will. God's grace is truly immense" (57:29). That sounds like an inclusive, broad understanding of God. A careful reading, however, suggests that Mohammad thinks the Christians and Jews believe they have "power over God's grace." It is as if Mohammad is pointing out that God has not forsaken those outside of the Judeo-Christian lineage.

My understanding is that Mohammad is appealing to Jews and Christians to accept his message as a continuation and correction of their religions. It seems to be a call for inclusion. However, in another place, the voice of the Qur'an sounds quite exclusive:

> Fight those People of the Book who do not
> truly believe in God and the Last Day, who
> do not forbid what God and His Messenger[33]

> have forbidden, who do not obey the rule of
> justice, until they pay the tax and agree to
> submit. The Jews said, "Ezra is the son of
> God," and the Christians said, "The Messiah
> is the son of God." ... May God confound
> them! How far astray they have been led!"
> (9:29–30)

In this reference, when Mohammad speaks of the tax, he is referring to the tax that is levied on all non-Muslims in those territories the Muslims have conquered.

While neither the Bible nor the Qur'an place a huge emphasis on punishment of sinners after death, both have some frightening warnings about what will happen to those who do not believe.

According to the Qur'an, "if he is one of those who denied the truth and went astray, he will be welcomed with scalding water. He will burn in Hell. This is the certain truth: [Prophet], glorify the name of your Lord the Supreme" (Qur'an 56:92–96). "Those who disbelieve among the People of the Book and the idolaters will have the Fire of Hell, there to remain. They are the worst of creation" (Qur'an 98:6).

The Bible has similar warnings. In the last book of the Hebrew Bible, which is scripture for both Jews and Christians: "'Surely the day is coming; it will burn like a furnace. All the arrogant and every evildoer will be stubble, and that day that is coming will set them on fire,' says the Lord Almighty" (Malachi 4:1). And in the last book of the Bible, "And I saw the dead, great and small, standing before the throne, and books were opened. ...

Then death and Hades were thrown into the lake of fire. The lake of fire is the second death. If anyone's name was not found written in the book of life, he was thrown into the lake of fire" (Revelation 20:12–15).

These are all written both as warnings to those within their religion to remain faithful and also to those who are unbelievers. Whether or not their true purpose is to coax unbelievers to repent and become believers, these passages also have the effect of deepening the divide between believers and those who do not believe.

One of the most loved sayings of Jesus is "I am the way and the truth and the life. No one comes to the Father except through me" (John 14:6). It is a word of invitation and comfort for Christians, and it is often read at funerals and memorial services. It is a comfort to the believer. Yet it is a very exclusive message for all those who do not put their faith in Jesus.

In each of these religions, the most conservative adherents place an emphasis on the most exclusive passages in their scriptures. The most liberal adherents emphasize the most inclusive passages, and they tend to gloss over or ignore the exclusive passages.

There is also the question of interpretation. The most liberal in each of the Abrahamic faiths will likely have no problem simply explaining that the exclusive passages in their scriptures need not be interpreted literally. One of my Christian friends commented to me concerning Jesus's words in what Christians call the Great Commission, which tells Jesus's followers to go into all the world and preach the gospel (see Matthew 28:18–20 and Mark 16:15–18) that Jesus never really said those words. I am fully aware of the fact that others of my Christian friends would consider her words to be nothing short of heresy and apostasy.

The hard question we must all wrestle with is this: What is God's intent? A number of years ago, it was popular to wear a bracelet with the letters WWJD. It was a reminder to ask oneself the question, "What would Jesus do?" I remember thinking then—and I still think—this is not always an easy question to answer. If you read the Bible carefully, you will discover that Jesus was a very complex teacher. His disciples, who were with him day in and day out for three years, often were completely perplexed by things he said. Another somewhat trite saying that was popular for a while was "Jesus is the answer." Of course, the smart retort often thrown about was this: "What's the question?"

The Gospel of Mark tells a story of a rich young man who approached Jesus and asked, "What must I do to inherit eternal life?" Jesus talked to the man about the commandments, and the man assured Jesus he had kept all of the commandments since he was a boy. Then Jesus looked at him and loved him and said, "One thing you lack. Go, sell everything you have and give to the poor, and you will have treasure in heaven." We're told the young man went away sad because he had great wealth. In the discussion between Jesus and his disciples that followed, once again perplexed by what Jesus said, they asked, "Who then can be saved?" (Mark 10:17–31).

Whenever we boil our religion down to something that fits on a bracelet or a bumper sticker, we run the danger of trivializing the depth and beauty and wisdom of our faith and its tradition. I believe that if we take our faith seriously, we need to look both at our own religion and to those of others with humility, admitting that it is just possible that we don't know it all. Humility admits that, even if we, like the young man who came to Jesus, have kept the commandments since childhood, and have prayed the prayers for our forgiveness and salvation, Jesus calls us to humble ourselves before him.

Christians are called to "humble yourself before the Lord" (James 4:10). Jews are told, "If my people, who are called by my name, will humble themselves and pray and seek my face and turn from their wicked ways, then will I hear from heaven and will forgive their sin and will heal their land" (2 Chronicles 7:14). Muslims are told, "Give good news to the humble whose hearts fill with awe whenever God is mentioned" (Qur'an 22:34–35). If Christians, Jews, and Muslims were to humble themselves before God and approach one another with a spirit of humility, perhaps we would find ourselves moving toward peace.

Thinking about the greatness of our God and the immensity of God's love for the world, is it not possible to imagine that God has enough love for even those who see God differently than we do?

Chapter 12

Immigrants and Refugees

Of my four grandparents, only one was born in the United States. One grandmother was born in Minnesota, her family having immigrated in the 1850s. The other three came to the United States in the early 1900s. All of them left Norway because it had become almost impossible to eke out a living. They came alone and dirt poor, as young single adults (or, in at least one case, as a teenager). At most, they had high school educations.

Their lives in America were not easy. They raised rather large families in rural Washington state. One of my grandfathers had a small farm where they raised chickens and berries—barely enough to sustain their eight children. The other grandfather was a fisherman, spending six months of every year fishing in Alaska, while his wife was at home with six children. Among my parents and aunts and uncles, there are hardly any college degrees—there simply was not enough money. Among my generation, however, almost all of us went to college and have enjoyed adequate incomes.

I sometimes ask myself why my grandparents came to America. Today, my relatives in Norway have comfortable lives in what has recently been named as the happiest country in the world. I know, however, that in the 1800s and early 1900s, Norway's rocky ground and fishing industry, which was my forebears' livelihood, could not sustain the population.

The conditions in Norway then, and other European countries as well, were probably not a whole lot different from conditions in rural and small-town Mexico today. My ancestors came with not much more than the clothes on their backs, traveling a long way without comfort, and often without any guarantees of what was ahead of them. Although their lives were not easy, they had several advantages over many of today's immigrants. First, they had white skin in a nation where virtually all of the power was in the hands of people with white skin. Second, they were Protestant Christians in a nation where the dominant religion was Protestant Christian. Third, they lived in a community where most of their neighbors' circumstances were very similar. Fourth, they were physically healthy. Fifth, although they had to learn English, their Norwegian language, like English, was a Germanic language, making it easier than, for example, going from Arabic or Chinese to English. Finally, and most certainly not least important, they were people of a deep faith that sustained them in every circumstance.

The Mexican immigrants I have met in recent years are working in low-paying jobs, and they work very hard to maintain their families. Most of them have about the same education opportunities that my grandparents had, and they hope their children will have better education opportunities in America. Like my grandparents, they came to the United States because, in their particular situations, earning a living was extremely difficult, and they hoped to find better opportunities here.

Most people in the world would probably prefer to stay in the places where they were born. Regardless of where it is, home is home. Most people don't pack up and move to a new country just for fun. Most immigrants move to a new country because they realize that their opportunities in their own countries are very limited, and there is another place where they have the possibility of a better future for themselves and their children.

Refugees have a similar but more extreme story in comparison with immigrants. Refugees live in countries where, because of war or famine or religious persecution or political turmoil, life has become extremely difficult or even impossible. Throughout human history, there have been both immigrants and refugees. Today, however, there is an official designation of refugee status determined by the United Nations High Commission for Refugees (UNCHR). Their website states, "We work to ensure that everybody has the right to seek asylum and find safe refuge, having fled violence, persecution, war or disaster at home."[34]

Although both immigrants and refugees suffer the pain and loneliness of leaving home and family and friends behind, there are big differences in their experiences. Some immigrants who are highly educated come to the US to work for companies like Microsoft or Amazon. At the other end of the spectrum are very poor immigrants who come to the US as migrants to do menial agricultural labor. Like immigrants, refugees can also have a variety of backgrounds.

Like the pages of history, the Bible has stories of many immigrants and refugees. When God called Abraham to leave his home and go to a place he would show him, Abraham became an emigrant (one who is leaving his or her homeland). When Abraham and Sarah sent Hagar and her son, Ishmael away, Hagar and Ishmael became refugees—people who had been cast out of their homeland. When Joseph's brothers sold him to a group of Ishmaelites, Joseph became a refugee. Later, when the Israelites fled from their life of slavery in Egypt, they were refugees, escaping from a life of violence and persecution.

The Israelite refugees wandered in the wilderness for forty years. When God gave them instructions through Moses, he reminded them of their past as a way of helping them understand how God would want them to treat others. "For the Lord your God is God of gods and Lord of lords. ... He defends the cause of the fatherless and the widow, and loves the alien, giving him food and clothing. And you are to love those who are aliens, for you yourselves were aliens in Egypt" (Deuteronomy 10:17–19).

These words from Moses also speak to us today. Unless you are a descendant of Native Americans, you trace your own family history back to someone who came to this country as an alien, a stranger, an immigrant, or a refugee. And if you are a Native American, you too may very well have been driven from your land against your choice. It's good for us to think about how it might have been for those who came before us. For some of us, the paths taken by our forebears were smooth and successful, but for others, life was rocky and difficult.

It is good for each of us to think about our own family stories and consider what challenges those who came before us met with—as well as the challenges our families might be dealing with today. Some of us come from very difficult situations. Others of us have had relatively easy lives. If you have always had a roof over your head and food on the table and clean water and access to education and the ability to live without fear, and in addition to all that have been free to worship as you choose, you are indeed a person of privilege.

At different times in history, there are migrations of people that generally have to do with either economic or political change. Today, we are experiencing a time of increased numbers of immigrants and refugees coming to the United States as well as other parts of the world. For most people, change is difficult. I like seeing people of all races and ethnicities in my city, but for many people, it's just not so easy.

Particularly in times of political upheaval in the world, the changes in the population can cause uneasiness and friction. Those who have been in a particular country, whether they trace their heritage in that country way back or have only been there for a generation or two, often see the newcomers as a threat.

Newcomers can be challenging. They don't always fit in. They bring with them their own traditions and ways of doing things. Sometimes they are seen as an economic burden on the country. In some places, it may seem that the newcomers are taking jobs.

On the other hand, imagine your city without Chinese food, Thai food, Mexican food, and so many more. Granted, we Scandinavians have still not been able to convince most of the world that lutefisk is delicious! Such a pity! In terms of the joy of diversity, my life has been greatly enriched by people of all races and ethnicities, and I would be very sorry to go back to the all-white world of my childhood.

Newcomers also come with their religious beliefs, and that can also be troubling to a nation that has often called itself a "Christian nation." Of course, whether or not this nation is or ever was a Christian nation is debatable. I am grateful that I live in a country that upholds religious liberty, giving me the right to worship as I please. I understand those who wish they could declare that this is a Christian nation and force everyone to become a Christian, but the reality is that there is no way that laws from any government can change people's hearts.

If we claim to be Christians, we have a mandate to welcome the stranger. As God told the Israelites through Moses, ours is a God who "loves the alien, giving him food and clothing." And not only are we to understand that God loves them, but we also are called to love them: "And you are to love those who are aliens, for your yourselves were aliens in Egypt" (Deuteronomy 10:19).

The words of Jesus are even stronger:

> When the Son of Man comes in his glory, and all the angels with him, he will sit on his glorious throne. All the nations will be gathered before him, and he will

separate the people one from another as a shepherd separates the sheep from the goats. He will put the sheep on his right and the goats on his left.

Then the King will say to those on his right, "Come, you who are blessed by my Father; take your inheritance, the kingdom prepared for you since the creation of the world. For I was hungry and you gave me something to eat, I was thirsty and you gave me something to drink, I was a stranger and you invited me in, I needed clothes and you clothed me, I was sick and you looked after me, I was in prison and you came to visit me."

Then the righteous will answer him, "Lord, when did we see you hungry and feed you, or thirsty and give you something to drink? When did we see you a stranger and invite you in, or needing clothes and clothe you? When did we see you sick or in prison and go to visit you?"

The King will reply, "Truly I tell you, whatever you did for one of the least of these brothers and sisters of mine, you did for me."

Then he will say to those on his left, "Depart from me, you who are cursed, into the eternal fire prepared for the devil and his angels. For I was hungry and you gave me nothing to eat, I was thirsty and you gave me nothing to drink, I was a stranger and you did not invite me in, I needed clothes and you did not clothe me, I was sick and in prison and you did not look after me."

They also will answer, "Lord, when did we see you hungry or thirsty or a stranger or needing clothes or sick or in prison, and did not help you?"

He will reply, "Truly I tell you, whatever you did not do for one of the least of these, you did not do for me."

Then they will go away to eternal punishment, but the righteous to eternal life. (Matthew 25:31–46)

The Bible does not mince words when it comes to how we are to treat the strangers among us. If we truly believe the Bible is the Word of God, we need to search our own hearts and think carefully about what God is calling us to do with regard to the strangers in our midst.

Chapter 13

Love Is the Only Possible Answer

We live in a world that can be dangerous. You might go to a lovely street fair in your city tomorrow, where you are enjoying a beautiful, sunny day and everyone is having a wonderful time. Suddenly, from out of nowhere, a truck loaded with explosives and commandeered by a suicide bomber plows into the crowd, killing and injuring dozens of people. Incidents like this are all too frequently in the news. It is terrifying.

It is terrifying, and that is exactly what terrorists want. We are, in fact, helpless in our quest to completely combat terrorism. We can increase our systems of security, but nothing can guarantee that there won't be someone with explosives who makes it past security onto a plane or into a crowd. Even the best surveillance cannot know everything. Often, it feels as if we live in a dangerous world. Since we see these things on the news day after day, it's natural for us to feel threatened.

Jesus also came into a world that experienced the fear of terrorism, albeit in a different form. Do you remember why Jesus's parents fled to Egypt when he was a baby? King Herod was so threatened by the fact that the Magi were looking for the one who was born king of the Jews that he put out a decree that all the boys in Bethlehem and its vicinity who were two years old and under be killed (Matthew 1:1–18). What a terrible, ruthless act of violence this was!

Jesus was born into a world where a despot had the power to snatch innocent children from their parents and have them put to death. Jesus died on the cross, condemned on false charges. In spite of being born into and having died in a violent, cruel world, his message was, and still is, that God loves this world. "For God so loved the world that he sent his one and only Son, that whoever believes in him shall not perish but have eternal life. For God did not send his Son into the world to condemn the world but to save the world through him" (John 3:16–17).

By no means am I arguing that, as Christians, we should simply accept violence and terrorism as the way the world is and allow the terrorists to do as they please. Everything possible should continue to be done to keep our world as safe as possible. But the reality is that violent extremists continue to pop up in unexpected places and commit heinous crimes against innocent people. This is a war we cannot win by simply bombing every corner of the world where there are terrorist sympathies, because, to be frank, we have been infiltrated. The ideology of Islamic terrorism has spread via cell groups and over the internet.

It is not limited to a certain geographical area, and it is not easy to contain.

Now, if you happen to work in counterespionage for the CIA or the FBI or ICE or TSA, for example, I want to thank you. I am very certain you have protected innocent citizens from would-be terrorist attacks, and you will continue to do so. We cannot simply lie down and allow terrorists to blow us to smithereens.

At the same time, we cannot be consumed by fear. Fear has the capacity to destroy us from within. Fear also has the power to cause us to do things that are just plain wrong. We don't have to go very far back in history to find stories of the mistreatment of American immigrants based on their nationalities in times of war. The Germans faced discrimination in the United States both during World War I and World War II. The Japanese were shipped off to internment camps during World War II. War arouses fear, and fear looks for ways to protect itself.

The problem is that when the war is over and we look back on how innocent people were mistreated because of their ethnicity or nationality, we realize that, most of the time, we were wrong. We allowed fear to overrule our better judgment. We lumped an entire people group together and found them guilty for the sins of their native lands. Since I wasn't around when these things happened, it's easy for me to point a finger and judge. Still, I wonder what we are doing today that will someday be seen as shortsighted and unwarranted.

There is always a certain amount of danger in this world. There is evil, and bad things happen. All of us—world and national leaders as well as individual citizens—make decisions every day based on our current understanding of the situations we face. I grew up knowing that the world could, at any time, be obliterated by nuclear weapons. It is a terrifying thought! So, what do we do? Do we live in fear? Do we look around at everyone with suspicion?

At this particular time in history, Muslims are the ones we fear most. Today, there are some 1.6 billion Muslims in the world and 3.3 million Muslims living in the United States. It is important for us to realize that countless Muslims, who simply want to live their lives peacefully, have been the victims of Islamic terrorism. The vast majority of Muslims today are just as troubled by the rise of Islamic terrorism as we are. Many, many Muslim refugees have fled their homelands because they were afraid of the terrorists. The vast majority of Muslim refugees hope and pray that Islamic terrorism will come to an end. They understand that many Americans look at them with suspicion, wondering whether or not they can be trusted.

I think that hate or war in the name of religion is one of the most heartbreaking things I can imagine. For Muslims to kill in the name of Allah—God—is horrendous. It represents a twisted, evil, extremist interpretation of the religion of Islam. I also think that we, as Christians, need to be very careful when we point our fingers at Muslims because we have in our history some heinous acts that were committed against people in the name of Christianity, often because of their religion. The vestiges of hate that grew out of those acts are still with us today.

The tragedy of the Holocaust, one of the most heinous acts in human history, did not simply arise out of nowhere with the rise of Hitler and the Nazis. Christian hatred toward Jews has infiltrated Christianity since the beginning, and it still lingers in many places today.

In our nation, the attitude toward black people, often sanctioned by Christians, is a shameful history that has left terrible scars on many, many people. It would be wonderful to be able to say that we have put racism behind us today, but unfortunately, racism rears its ugly head in our nation again and again and again. And again.

For Christians to believe they have the right to hate anyone at all because of their nationality, race, skin color, religion, economic condition, sexual identity, or any other reason is simply sin. When we look at any group of people and speak with disdain about "those people" or harbor hatred in our heart toward "those people," we are guilty of sin against humanity and against God, who created us and "those people" as well.

Every one of us needs to examine our hearts because these sorts of prejudices can be so insidious that we don't even realize we have them. The first thing we need to do is acknowledge the fact that we might have some blind spots with respect to our fellow humans. The Bible says, "Anyone who claims to be in the light but hates his brother (or sister) is still in the darkness" (1 John 2:9). "If we claim to be without sin, we deceive ourselves and the truth is not in us. If we confess our sins, he is faithful and just and will forgive us our sins and purify us from all unrighteousness" (1 John 1:8–9).

The good news is that, in Christ, we can stop hating. We can choose to love. Loving is so freeing. Think about the people you have known who simply love everyone.

They are the happiest people on earth. Think about people you have known who are filled with hatred. They're not very happy, are they? Love is not only good because it is what God commands; it is good for your physical and mental and emotional health. Of course, it is also good for the world!

Perhaps you are thinking, *Yes, but.* "Yes, but surely God doesn't expect us to love terrorists?" That is a hard question. It is true that the Bible includes some troubling words about hate, but here's what Jesus said about that: "You *have heard* that it was said, 'Love your neighbor and hate your enemy.' *But I tell you*: Love your enemies and pray for those who persecute you, that you may be sons of your Father in heaven" (Matthew 5:43–45). Jesus calls on us to be different because of God's love for us.

There is one more very important reason we need to love our Muslim brothers and sisters. In the final analysis, love is the only possible answer. We cannot rid the world of Muslims. We cannot simply send them all back to where they came from. We cannot convince all Muslims to become Christians. The reality is that love is our only hope. And the only kind of love that is our hope is the radical love of Jesus Christ, who gave his life on the cross as an atonement for our sins and the sins of all—yes all!— the world.

The message of the cross is that God's love is big enough for the entire world. We who have received the gift of God's love are called to love others, just as we have been loved. This does not mean that we are simply to love the people who think the way we do or look the way we do. We cannot simply love people we happen to like. This love that God calls us to is a radical choice to love even those who hate us.

Love benefits not just the loved, but the lover. When we truly love with God's love, we will not be afraid.

> There is no fear in love. But perfect love drives out fear. ... We love because he first loved us. If anyone says "I love God," yet hates his brother, he is a liar. ... And he has given us this command: Whoever loves God must also love his brother. (1 John 4:18–21)

It is helpful to remember that, while love can be a feeling, it can also be an action. Love can be an action taken by choice. You do not need to feel all warm and fuzzy in order to love someone. You don't need to agree with someone in order to love them. You don't even need to like people in order to love them. The kind of love that God demonstrates is different from the love that comes and goes according to our whims. God's love is eternal and beyond measure. It is only when we meditate on the love we have received in Christ Jesus that we can, through the power of the Holy Spirit, extend love to all. "God demonstrates his own love for us in this: While we were still sinners, Christ died for us" (Romans 5:8).

Some people are easy to love, and others are not. God calls us to love all of them anyway. Those of us who have received the love of Christ Jesus need to remember that our salvation was never based on our goodness or on our being loveable. Our salvation is only by God's grace, extended to us with love. Love is not an option. As

Christians, God has loved us and called us to a life filled with the love of God. We love, not in our own strength, but through Christ.

> We love because he first loved us. Whoever claims to love God yet hates a brother or sister is a liar. For whoever does not love their brother and sister, whom they have seen, cannot love God, whom they have not seen. And he has given us this command: Anyone who loves God must also love their brother and sister. (1 John 4:19–20)

For some, who have suffered greatly because of Islamic aggression and terrorism, the task of loving is immensely challenging. I think, for example, of my friend, Maurice. Maurice is a Syrian Christian who had to flee from his native land and is now living in Sweden. Think, for a minute, about his native country. Syria has been home to many Christians since the first century AD. It's hard to even imagine how painful it has been for Syrian Christians to see their homeland largely destroyed and this place of their Christian history become a place where Christians are persecuted. Pray for Syrian Christians who have suffered so much.

It is absolutely true that some people are very difficult to love. The only way we can begin to love them is to grasp the amazing love we have received from God. "How great is the love the Father has lavished on us, that we should be called children of God! And that is what we are!" (1 John 3:1). When we receive and focus on God's unconditional love for us, we can, in turn, love our neighbors. Even the neighbors who have wronged us most.

Chapter 14

What Can We Do?

As I learned to sing many years ago in Sunday school, "This little light of mine, I'm gonna let it shine ... 'til Jesus comes." Let's think not about how impossible this giant is and not about how much we can't do. Let's think about some things we can do.

It is essential that we begin with a spirit of humility. The problem of hatred in our world today is overwhelming. The more you study and listen and read, the more you will be alarmed. It is true that the problems are enormous. You and I can't solve everything, but we can do something. We can be humble. Think first about this beautiful passage in Philippians, which describes Jesus:

> Therefore if you have any encouragement from being united with Christ, if any comfort from his love, if any common sharing in the Spirit, if any tenderness and compassion, then make my joy complete by being like-minded, having the same love, being one in spirit and of one mind. Do

nothing out of selfish ambition or vain conceit. Rather, in humility value others above yourselves, not looking to your own interests but each of you to the interests of the others.

In your relationships with one another, have the same mind-set as Christ Jesus: Who, being in very nature God, did not consider equality with God something to be used to his own advantage; rather, he made himself nothing by taking the very nature of a servant, being made in human likeness. And being found in appearance as a man, he humbled himself by becoming obedient to death— even death on a cross! (Philippians 2:1–8)

If Jesus acted in humility, how much more should we act in humility? There were evil powers in the world when Jesus walked the earth, but Jesus never taught his followers to return evil for evil. Going out and ranting and raving about the evils of Islamic terrorism is not going to solve anything. Neither is staying home and harboring hatred toward your Muslim neighbor.

If you would like to take some action, start with a thorough examination of your own heart. Begin by praying, "Search me, O God, and know my heart; test me and know my anxious thoughts. See if there is any offensive way in me, and lead me in the way everlasting" (Psalm 139:23–24). If you have hardness in your heart toward others, ask God to forgive you and soften your heart.

Be sure to pray. Pray for the Muslims living in the United States—and particularly for the Muslims living in your community. As you pray, ask God to help you to love them and to understand them. Pray for Muslims around the world who are hated because of their religion. Pray for Muslims who are refugees, fleeing from the war-torn parts of the world that once were their homes. Pray for Muslims who have been the victims of Islamic terrorism in their own countries. Pray for Christians who hate Muslims just because they are Muslims. Pray for Christians who hate women who wear their head coverings when they go out in public. Pray for the church, that Christians might seek God's wisdom concerning their Muslim neighbors. Pray that we Christians will not be consumed by hatred. Pray for the terrorists—lost souls searching for meaning in a world they do not understand and claiming allegiance to Allah, who they certainly do not understand. Pray again for yourself, that your heart would be pure.

If you have Muslims in your community, look for ways of getting to know them. Depending on your circumstances and your community, this may be rather easy or quite difficult. I'm a natural introvert, and it's not easy for me to just introduce myself to strangers. Sometimes, however, that is exactly what God calls us to do. One thing that actually helps is that most Muslim women will wear headscarves, so it's pretty obvious who they are. One tiny little thing you can do is simply smile when you meet a woman wearing the headscarf (hijab) since she already realizes that many people look upon her with disdain.

Look for opportunities. If you're standing in line next to a Muslim, you might make casual, friendly conversation.

Hold it! Warning to men! The friendly smile to a Muslim woman might not be best coming from you! In most cases, Muslim women will not be comfortable talking to men who are not their relatives. In many Muslim cultures, Muslim women are not even allowed to look at a man who is not part of their family. Also, women, do not offer to shake hands with a Muslim man, since he is not allowed to touch a woman who is not his family member. Likewise, Muslim men will not be likely to strike up a conversation with a woman who is not a relative. Sometimes, modern, more liberal Muslim men will extend their hand to a woman for a handshake, and in that case, you are safe to shake hands. But just be very careful to be sensitive and watch for the body language of the person you are approaching.

In many cases, if there is a mosque in your community, you would be welcome to visit. It's good to recognize the fact, however, that there is a wide range in Islam, from rather liberal to ultra conservative. Start by not making any assumptions. If you would like to visit, call the mosque and ask if they allow non-Muslims to visit, and if so, ask when it would be convenient for you to come. Explain to them that you are a Christian who is interested in learning more about Islam and meeting your Muslim neighbors. You should know that in all mosques, you will be expected to remove your shoes upon entering. If you are a woman, you will be expected to wear some sort of scarf to cover your hair. Among more conservative Muslims, the head covering needs to cover every bit of your hair. And, of course, your clothing should be modest. All of this is a matter of respect.

When you approach Muslims, don't do it with the motive of converting them to Christianity. Rather, approach them with respect, understanding that they have the right to believe as they choose, which is usually what they have been taught from birth. It is perfectly fine if, in your heart, you pray they will become Christians. But if you truly want to reach out to them in love, you must begin by being respectful of their religion and their way of life.

I remember a time when a new family moved into our neighborhood. They were a family with several kids, and the woman and I were young stay-at-home moms. She was so kind and friendly to me. One day, she brought me some of her homemade jam and invited our family to join them for dinner. We went and enjoyed ourselves. After dinner, they asked us if we would watch a video with them, which we did. It quickly became apparent that they were trying to convert us to their religion. We kindly explained to them that we were Christians, happy and active in our church, and that nothing they might say could possibly cause us to change. After that, she dropped me like a lead balloon. Our friendship was over. I share this because it taught me a lesson about how it can feel to be on the other side of evangelism. I realized that, in her mind, our friendship was only valid if we would join their religion. That's not true friendship, is it?

When you reach out in friendship to Muslims, do it with no strings attached. You are not selling a used car. You are not even called to change them. If God chooses to change their hearts, God will do so. Your responsibility is simply to love them with the humility of Jesus.

In addition to friendship, you can give financially. There are wonderful organizations that are helping refugees around the world, and the generosity of Christians is greatly needed. Give as generously as you are able to agencies that are working with refugees. Their task is not easy. The needs are great—sometimes enormously overwhelming—and the resources are limited. Think about the many blessings you enjoy and ask yourself how your generosity might encourage both the workers and the refugees they serve.

If you have refugees in your own community, there are certainly needs among them. Most refugees have had to leave terrible situations where their lives were in danger. They come to this country with nothing much at all. Many of them have lost everything. In many cases, the things they have gone through are almost unimaginable. Take some time to think about what it must be like for them. Think about what might be especially difficult for them in your community. Imagine how you would feel if you were in their shoes. Find out what is being done to help refugees near you and see if there are ways you can join in.

Surprisingly, one of my favorite passages concerning giving is from the Old Testament book of Leviticus.

> When you reap the harvest of your land,
> do not reap to the very edges of your field
> or gather the gleanings of your harvest. Do
> not go over your vineyard a second time or
> pick up the grapes that have fallen. Leave

them for the poor and the foreigner. I am
the Lord your God. (Leviticus 19:9–10)

I don't have any fields—I don't even have a vegetable garden—but I have been blessed with certain resources. The way I understand this passage of scripture is that I must not keep everything I have for myself, whether it is my money, my time, or my abilities. When it says not to reap to the very edges of your field, it means don't take everything you can get and keep it for yourself. Enjoy your crops—but also leave something to provide for the needy. And by the way, did you notice that, in this passage, scripture again reminds us to care for the foreigner? It is very clear in the Bible that God cares about the poor and the foreigner. If God has blessed you with financial resources, remember that God expects you to share some of what you have with those who are less fortunate than you.

Another way you can help your Muslim brothers and sisters, whether they are rich or poor, is to be an advocate on their behalf. When you hear people make unkind remarks about Muslims, you may have opportunities to respectfully disagree. This is definitely not always easy, and there may be times when your only choice is to simply ignore the remark. Other times, however, it can be good to engage the person in conversation. Ask them to explain. Mention the fact that many, many Muslims in many parts of the world today are victims of Islamic terrorism. You could simply say that you can imagine that if we think *we* want peace, imagine how difficult it must be for Muslims who want peace and realize that they themselves are hated because of what other Muslims are doing in the name of their religion, Islam.

If fellow Christians, particularly in your faith community, speak hatefully about Muslims, I think this is the best place for you to engage them in conversation. Just mention the fact that Jesus taught us to love our neighbors, and he never stipulated that those neighbors had to be Christians in order for us to love them.

> Jesus said, "You have heard that it was said, 'Love your neighbor and hate your enemy.' But I tell you, love your enemies and pray for those who persecute you, that you may be children of your Father in heaven. He causes his sun to rise on the evil and the good, and sends rain on the righteous and the unrighteous. If you love those who love you, what reward will you get? Are not even the tax collectors doing that? And if you greet only your own people, what are you doing more than others? Do not even pagans do that?" (Matthew 5:43–47)

This is a very difficult time to be a Muslim. We who call ourselves Christians need to recognize the pain they are suffering in so very many places around the world—and even in our own communities. Quite honestly, in many places, their civilizations are in shambles. I think one thing we can do is look for ways in which we can simply sit beside them.

By sitting beside them, I mean becoming their friend and advocate. To sit beside people can be as simple as very literally sitting next to them. When I was in fifth or sixth grade, I noticed a little girl—probably a first grader—crying on a bottom stair at school. I went over, sat down next to her, and comforted her. It was a small action that took very little on my part, and I never thought about it again. That is, until, some forty years later, when I ran into one of my classmates from that time. She said, "I still remember the time you went and sat down on the stairs with that little girl who was crying. You were so kind." I was dumbfounded that she remembered, but as soon as she mentioned it, I remembered it too.

As I thought about it, I realized that some of the best things I have done for others has been simply to sit beside them in whatever they are dealing with. I also realized that there have been too many times when I have just walked away from those who needed a friend to sit beside them.

Do you remember what Job's friends did when he was suffering such immense pain? "They sat on the ground with him for seven days and seven nights. No one said a word to him, because they saw how great his suffering was" (Job 2:13). As the story went on, those friends didn't always get it right. And neither will we. But let's at least be determined to do what we can.

Chapter 15

Receiving Muslim Hospitality

There are how many Muslims in the world? Somewhere around 1.6 billion! So, it would be outrageously presumptuous for me—or anyone, for that matter—to say this is what Muslims are like. I would, however, like to introduce you to some Muslims in my community.

Jawad is a leader in his community, and he is one of the first we got to know. He is a retired Microsoft employee who lives in a lovely home with his wife. They have three adult children who often visit them. They are from Iran, and they are Shii Muslims. They have welcomed us into their home and into their mosque on several occasions. When my husband had some health concerns, Jawad said, "Please! If you ever need help, you can call me anytime, day or night, and I will come and help!" He's a very good neighbor.

Tezcan is a Sunni Muslim from Turkey. He is married and has two young children. He is highly committed to interfaith initiatives, and having gotten to know us and our similar interests, he makes sure to invite us to interfaith events. At our invitation, Tezcan also attended a worship service at our church.

When most Christians think about Muslims, we tend to think about reaching out to them with the love of Jesus and perhaps even leading them to Christ. This is an admirable goal, and it is certainly appropriate in some situations. Humility, however, may require that we allow our Muslim neighbors to reach out to us. Sometimes, we need to be open to allowing them to extend hospitality to us. Particularly with Muslims, hospitality is highly important.

As I write this, the Muslim month of Ramadan has just ended. The Islamic lunar calendar has 354 or 355 days and twelve months in a year. Because this differs from the Gregorian calendar's year of 365 or 366 days, Ramadan gradually, ten days at a time, moves through the seasons. This year, Ramadan ran from May 26 to June 24. Every year, Ramadan comes ten days earlier than the year before, compared with the Gregorian calendar.

During Ramadan, all Muslims, worldwide, observe a fast from sunrise to sunset. During their fast, they do not eat, drink (including water), smoke, or engage in sexual relations. Children who have not reached puberty are not included in the fast. There are also exceptions for those who are traveling, menstruating, ill, pregnant, or breastfeeding.

At sunset, they gather together to break the fast and eat a meal, called an Iftar dinner. My husband and I had the privilege of being invited to three Iftar dinners this year. Because Ramadan this year was at the time when the days are longest, the hour of breaking the fast did not come until 9:11 p.m. in our time zone. For each evening, the arrival time was earlier, allowing for a time of visiting and, in two cases, programs.

The first Iftar dinner we attended was held at Seattle University. We were pleased to find ourselves seated with two young women, Havva and Safiye. One of them was working on her PhD in computer science at the University of Washington. The other was a researcher at Microsoft. They were both single and wonderful dinner companions. I asked them about the difficulty of fasting, and they responded that they like it because it reminds them that they are strong.

The second Iftar dinner was in the home of a young couple, Erdem and Kubra. We enjoyed a lively conversation with them, particularly because their adorable two-year-old son jabbered away for us in Turkish. What a charming family! They explained that one of their traditions was to break the fast by first eating dates, as the prophet Mohammad always did.

The third Iftar dinner was held in our own church, and my husband and I attended as representatives of the church. About six months ago, a mosque in Bellevue, Washington, was the target of arson. The building was partially destroyed, and they are in the process of planning and rebuilding, so they had no place to hold a community Iftar dinner, and asked to use our building. They wanted this dinner to be a thank you to the city officials, including the firefighters and police who responded to the incident and helped them. The event started at seven o'clock, and during that time, they had a program, inviting officials from the police, fire department, and city to speak. They also made a presentation about their Muslim beliefs. Because many of those attending were not Muslims, and therefore not fasting, they provided appetizers for their guests. I must say, it is humbling to sit at the table with food and drink while others at the table, who have had nothing to eat or drink all day, are fasting. Finally, at 9:11 p.m., everyone was able to eat and drink.

At our table, we got to know a man from Egypt who is a professor of engineering at the University of Washington, and his son, Omar, who is a sixth grader. Omar has a beautiful smile and a twinkle in his eye, and was truly fun to talk with. He loves math, and my guess is that he's a very good student.

Muslims also pray five times a day. At the first, and largest Iftar dinner, the call to evening prayer was announced, and most of the Muslim men left the room to go and pray in a separate room. At the second dinner, which was in a home, the husband and wife each briefly excused themselves, and went into another room to pray. At the last Iftar dinner, we met in our church's large all-purpose room. They played a recording of the call to prayer, and all of the Muslim men went to a corner of the room and lined up shoulder to shoulder in rows facing east and observed the prayer time together.

It was interesting for me to watch this group of Muslims praying in my own church. I think God would be pleased, but I am not sure how some of our congregation would have reacted had they been there. If we are to continue to have interfaith gatherings, we need to talk about these things ahead of time since it might be difficult for many people. My own belief is that God hears the prayers of all people, including those who pronounce his name "Allah," but I realize not all Christians agree with me.

That evening, we also met a Sudanese man who has been educated in the US and is starting a company that will use solar power to bring clean water to West and East Africa, in an attempt to eradicate waterborne diseases such as cholera and diarrheal infections. He wants to go back to his own people and help them.

One thing I have learned from these Muslims and others I have encountered is that they are eager to tell their side of the story. They are fully aware of the anti-Muslim sentiments that are common in the news. They are fully aware of the horrors of Islamic extremism, and many of them have come to the United States hoping to escape the dangers of terrorism. For many of them, their homelands have changed drastically. The political landscape in predominantly Muslims nations has been so unsettled. Some of them have left their homelands because they fear the changes taking place. Others have been literally driven from their homelands by war and destruction.

When they come here, they are looking for safety and an opportunity to live their lives in peace. They have heard that Americans believe in freedom of religion, and they are hoping that includes them. They want to be known and understood as good people who simply want to live in peace.

One way we can love and honor them is by receiving their hospitality. If you have the honor of being invited to a mosque or to the home of a Muslim, accept the invitation and go. Watch carefully so you don't offend your hosts and receive their hospitality as graciously as you possibly can. Know that hospitality is a very important value in many parts of the Muslim world.

Chapter 16

The Tenacity of Hope

Gentle reader, if you have read this far, you may be experiencing a feeling of despair over the immensity of the problem of hatred in our world. Let me assure you that I have felt that despair. As I have been writing, I have also been listening and reading and learning, and there is, indeed, some very bad news in the world today. It would be so easy to simply throw up our hands and say there is nothing we can do except to wait for the Lord to return.

But stop for a moment and think. If you and I think we are troubled by the things going on in our world, just imagine how God feels. God loves this world more than we can ever imagine. Jesus did not come into the world to live among us and die for us because we were good. Rather, he came, and still comes today, because we cannot save ourselves. Those of us who have received his gift of salvation have so much for which to be grateful. However, we must never begin to think that our salvation is something we have earned or that we deserve. Christ died for us *while we were still sinners* (Romans 5:8).

That Christ died for us while we were still sinners means that Christ also died for other people who are still sinners. The love we see in Jesus's sacrifice for our sins is the love that God feels for every single person on the face of the earth. God's love and mercy are for all people. That is why we who have tasted of God's love and mercy must, in turn, show love and mercy to others. Just as God's love for us is not conditional on our goodness or even our acknowledgement, so our love for others must also be unconditional.

Our love for Muslims, or for anyone at all, is not conditional on their appreciation of our efforts. It is not dependent on how good or nice or polite or agreeable they are. It is not dependent on what we think of their religion. It is not conditional on their acceptance of our understanding of God or of salvation. We are called simply to love our neighbors. In fact, the Bible tells us to love your neighbor as yourself! Really? Love them as myself? Yes! Love your neighbor as yourself (Leviticus 19:18; Matthew 19:19; Matthew 22:39; Mark 12:31, 33; Luke 10:27; Romans 13:9; Galatians 5:14; James 2:8). When something as central as the way we treat our neighbor comes up in scripture over and over, we need to pay attention! We need to understand that God has something to say to us that we do not dare ignore.

Following the Bible's teachings that we are to love our neighbor and even our enemies is not easy. It does not necessarily come naturally. Love in this case is an action verb. You may or may not have loving feelings toward your neighbors, but regardless of how you feel about those people, the Bible says you must love them. Imagine, for just a moment, what the world would be like if everyone were to live this way! It would be a wonderful world, wouldn't it?

Now, think about the world as you know it. It's pretty obvious that the world is seriously lacking when it comes to love. How about Christians? Could we imagine what the world would be like if all Christians were to truly love their neighbors? Even the ones who are different? Even the ones they disagree with?

Maybe you're thinking, *I can't do that.* The truth is, in your own strength, you can't. But scripture demands that we love, so it must be possible. I challenge you to get a concordance and read all of the references in the Bible that have the word *love."* There are so many!

I truly believe that love is the only answer for our world. I also believe that we cannot afford to give up. We are called to be people of hope. "And hope does not disappoint us, because God has poured out his love into our hearts, by the Holy spirit, whom he has given us" (Romans 5:5).

It would be easy for us to say the world is just a mess and there's nothing we can do that makes a difference. That is hopelessness. The Bible teaches us not to give up. "Let us not become weary in doing good, for at the proper time we will reap a harvest if we do not give up" (Galatians 6:9). As Christians, we are called to be people of love and of hope.

We are living in a time when hope seems to have been replaced with fear and animosity. Hope, in the face of a world that seems to be moving toward self-annihilation, is certainly audacious. Hope that is not only audacious, but also tenacious, is not easy. What does it mean to hope when the world seems to have so many seemingly hopeless situations?

When we think about all of the evils in our world, it is easy to focus on how we as a nation can defend ourselves and how we can keep the world safe. The reality is that we cannot guarantee our own—or anyone else's—safety in every circumstance. I am not at all opposed to safety measures or defensive military strength. We, as a nation, should do everything we can to make our world safe. Yet, we are wise to understand that even the best surveillance and the best military power cannot fully ensure our safety. That is why we must ultimately put our faith in God. I like the way the psalmist puts it: "Some trust in chariots and some in horses, but we trust in the name of the Lord our God" (Psalm 20:7).

We put our hope, not in what we can do, but in what God can do. Our calling is to love God and love our neighbor, and to place our hope and trust in God. God also calls us to prayer. It is in prayer that we express our dependence on God, and it is in the act of praying that God calms our fears and teaches us how to love. "How great is the love the Father has lavished on us, that we should be called children of God! And that is what we are!" (1 John 3:1). We have so much to be thankful for—most of all, God's amazing, boundless, eternal love. "So then, just as you have received Christ Jesus, continue to live in him" (Colossians 2:6).

Look once more at the picture of Adam, grieving over the death of his son, Abel, and the sin of his son, Cain. Adam's heart must have been breaking. The hatred of one of his sons for the other resulted in Abel's murder and Cain's guilt.

Could there have been a better solution? Did the jealousy Cain felt over Abel's sacrifice mean there could be no reconciliation in their relationship? They both brought sacrifices before God. Perhaps Cain and Abel could have learned from each other. Perhaps Cain and Abel could have come to love each other.

As I look at that painting, I see, in Adam, a picture of God, mourning over the enmity between his children. Our great and loving God bends over his children and weeps. God's immense, loving, heart breaks when we choose to hate and destroy one another. "See what great the love the Father has lavished on us, that we should be called children of God! And that is what we are!" (1 John 3:1). "Dear friends, since God so loved us, we also ought to love one another" (1 John 4:11).

Endnotes

1   "The 1951 Convention Relating to the Status of Refugees and its 1967 Protocol," accessed September 8, 2017, https//www.unhcr. org/en-us/4ec262df9.pdf#zoom=95.

2   A. A. Milne, *Winnie-the-Pooh.*

3   John L. Esposito, *What Everyone Needs to Know About Islam* (New York: Oxford University Press, 2002), 45, 47.

4   Pew Forum on Religion and Public Life.

5   Justo L. Gonzalez, *The Story of Christianity: The Early Church to the Dawn of the Reformation, Volume I,* San Francisco: Harper, 1984, 30.

6   Gonzalez, 248–9.

7   The Qur'an 2:256.

8   The Qur'an 9:29.

9   Esposito, 71.

10 Gonzalez, 249–250.

11 Goddard, Hugh. *A History of Christian-Muslim Relations.* Chicago: New Amsterdam Books, 200. 82.

12 Goddard, 91–92.

13 To read more about this, see *The Looming Tower* and *The Terror Years,* by Lawrence Wright.

14 "Terrorist attacks and related incidents in the United States," accessed September 8, 2017, www.johnstonsarchive.net.

15 Bruce Hoffman, *Inside Terrorism,* (Columbia University Press, 2006), 22.

16 WorldAtlas.com.

17 https://en.wikipedia.org/wiki/Sayyid_Qutb

18 Sayyid Qutb, *Milestones,* in *The Sayyid Qutb Reader,* Albert J. Bergesen, Ed., (Routledge, 2008), 37.

19 Ibid., 39.

20 Ibid., 59.

21 Ibid., 64.

22 Ibid., 81.

23 Ibid., 151–152.

24 Ibid., 154.

25 Ibid., 159.

26 Longfellow, Henry Wadsworth "Christmas Bells," Henry Wadsworth Longfellow [online resource], Maine Historical Society, Accessed February 28, 2017. http://www.hwlongfellow.org

27 cms.cityoftacoma.org

28 Franklin H. Littell, *The Crucifixion of the Jews,* Macon, Georgia: Mercer University Press, 1986, 106–7.

29 Rudolf Hoess, *Commandant of Auschwitz: The Autobiography of Rudolf Hoess.* Cleveland: World Publishing Co., 1959, 32.

30 Littell, 108.

31 In the Qur'an, "God speaks directly to people and to the Prophet, often using 'We,' the first-person plural of majesty, to represent Himself" (Introduction to The Qur'an, Oxford University Press, xx).

32 In the Qur'an, "We" is the voice of Allah.

33 By "His Messenger," the Qur'an means Mohammad.

34 http://www.unhcr.org/

Bibliography

Chittister, Joan. *The Tent of Abraham*. Beacon Press, 2006

Daniel, Ben. *The Search for Truth About Islam*. Westminster John Knox Press, 2013.

Doyle, Tom. *Dreams and Visions*. Thomas Nelson, 2012.

Esposito, John L. *What Everyone Needs to Know About Islam*. New York: Oxford University Press, 2002.

Fretheim, Terence E. *Abraham: Trials of Family and Faith*. Columbia, SC: The University of South Carolina Press, 2007.

Ghobash, Omar Saif. *Letters to a Young Muslim*. Picador, 2017.

Goddard, Hugh. *A History of Christian-Muslim Relations*. Chicago: New Amsterdam Books, 2000.

Gonzalez, Justo L. *The Story of Christianity, Volume 1*. San Francisco: Harper Collins, 1984.

Griffith, Sidney H. *The Church in the Shadow of the Mosque: Christians and Muslims in the World of Islam*. Princeton, NJ: Princeton University Press, 2008.

Haddad, Yvonne Yazbeck, Jane I. Smith, and Kathleen M. Moore. *Muslim Women in America: The Challenge of*

Islamic Identity Today. New York: Oxford University Press: 2006.

Haleem, M.A.S. Abdel. trans. *The Qur'an*. New York: Oxford University Press, 2008.

Hoess, Rudolf. *Commandant of Auschwitz: The Autobiography of Rudolf Hoess*. Cleveland: World Publishing Co., 1959.

Hoffman, Bruce. *Inside Terrorism*. Columbia University Press, 2006.

Idliby, Ranya. *The Faith Club*. Free Press, 2006.

Jenkins, Phillip. *God's Continent: Christianity, Islam, and Europe's Religious Crisis*. Oxford University Press, 2007.

Longfellow, Henry Wadsworth "Christmas Bells" Henry Wadsworth Longfellow [online resource], Maine Historical Society, Accessed February 28, 2017. http://www.hwlongfellow.org

Littell, Franklin H. *The Crucifixion of the Jews*. Mercer University Press, 1986.

Mackenzie, Don. *Religion Gone Astray: What We Found at the Heart of Interfaith*. Skylight Paths, 2011.

Medearis, Carl. *Muslims, Christians, and Jesus*. Bethany House, 2008.

Milne, A. A., *Winnie-the-Pooh*. Dutton, 1961, c. 1926.

Mishra, Pankaj. *Age of Anger: A History of the Present*. Farrar, Straus and Giroux, 2017

Moucarry, Chawkat. *The Prophet and the Messiah: An Arab Christian's Perspective on Islam & Christianity*. InterVarsity Press, 2001.

Mudge, Lewis S. *The Gift of Responsibility: The Promise of Dialogue among Christians, Jews, and Muslims.* New York: Continuum, 2008.

Nasr, Seyyed Hossein. *Islam: Religion, History and Civilization.* New York: HarperOne, 2002.

Pearson, Carlton. *God is Not a Christian, Nor A Jew, Muslim, Hindu.* Atria Books, 2010.

Qutb, Sayyid. *Milestones,* in *The Sayyid Qutb Reader,* Albert J. Bergesen, Ed, Routledge, 2008.

Siljander, Mark D., *A Deadly Misunderstanding.* HarperOne, 2008.

Spencer, Robert. *Religion of Peace? Why Christianity Is and Islam Isn't.* Regnery Publishers, 2007.

_____ *Islam Unveiled: Disturbing Questions About the World's Fastest-growing Faith.* Encounter Books, 2002.

Taber, Shirin. *Muslims Next Door.* Zondervan, 2004.

Trousdale, Jerry. *Miraculous Movements: How Hundreds of Thousands of Muslims are Falling in Love with Jesus.* Thomas Nelson, 2012.

Volf, Miroslav. *Allah.* New York: Harper One, 2011.

_____. *Exclusion and Embrace.* Nashville, TN: Abingdon Press, 1996.

Wright, Lawrence. *The Looming Tower.* Alfred A. Knopf, 2006.

_____. *The Terror Years.* Alfred A. Knopf, 2016.

Printed in the United States
By Bookmasters